BREAKING FREE

A compilation of short stories on mental illness and ways to handle them

BY MICHAEL CASEY

Orla Kelly Publishing,
27 Kilbrody, Mount Oval,
Rochestown Cork

For everyone out there who are fighting monsters unbeknownst to the world...

Disclaimer:

The illnesses portrayed in this book are just examples of how a mental illness can reveal itself to the world. They are **not** the only way someone can suffer from one. Mental illness affects everyone differently. If you feel that you can relate to any of the stories in this book and may have a mental illness, I advise you to go to a doctor and get a professional opinion.

There is nothing more powerful than the human mind. It can create planes to fly across the world and build skyscrapers so high that they stand amongst the clouds. It can write awe-inspiring books, paint magnificent pictures and play breath-taking music. It can win Nobel prizes and give people the belief that they can be anyone they want to be and do anything they want to do in life. It can change the world.

The human mind is capable of many great and amazing things. But it is also capable of enduring a lot of suffering and hardships. Fear, doubt and self-hatred, are all emotions people endure every single day. Pain is a part of life, and it is natural and necessary for personal growth. What is not natural is hiding this pain. It is not right to hide your pain and pretend to yourself that everything's okay when your mind is giving you a sign that you need help.

So, I ask you as you're about to read this book, if you were experiencing mental health issues would you speak out and ask for help? Or would you hide your suffering from the world and go on with your life as though nothing was wrong, and everything was okay?

Contents

Self-Harm

❖

Merlyn's Story

She screams and shouts and punches the wall,
But to stand back up, first she must fall.

Merlyn was a talented young girl who was the apple of her mother's eye and Daddy's little girl. She lived life with a sense of wonder and would always be seen with a smile. She loved to dance, and she loved to sing. "When I grow up, I'm going to be a famous singer!" she would say. "Everyone will be singing my songs!"

One day, Merlyn came home from school and was sad for no reason. She had had a good day in school, so she didn't know why she was so sad. "It's a beautiful day outside. I'm supposed to be out there enjoying myself in the garden. I'm supposed to be having the time of my life. So why am I so sad?" she asked herself.

1

The next day when Merlyn came home, she was sad again for no reason. She was sad the day after that, and the day after that. Eventually she came home from school feeling sad every day! She was spending her time in her room alone, crying every day and wishing she could just be happy again. She was beginning to hate herself for being sad all the time and had started to take her low moods out on her mam and dad by shouting at them. She was sad and angry at the same time, and she didn't know why.

Merlyn began to spend more and more time in her room. The only company she had were her toys on her bed. But even they weren't enough to stop her from getting sad and angry. One day, she looked at one of her teddy bears and screamed at the top of her lungs. She picked up the teddy and threw it against the wall. Then she picked it up and tugged on its arm as hard as she could. She pulled, and she pulled until it came off!

Merlyn looked at her toy and couldn't believe what she had just done – she had torn it in two! She felt guilty, because she had just destroyed one of her most treasured possessions, but at the same time she felt a little relieved. Merlyn's heart was racing, and she was panting. Suddenly she didn't feel sad or angry anymore. She went to bed and slept through the whole night.

The next night, Merlyn felt sad again as she sat alone in the silence of her room. Tears slowly started running down her soft cheeks and she brushed them away with her hands. She didn't want to feel like this. Suddenly, she grabbed a book from the book shelf and threw it against the door. She picked up the lamp on her bedside table and flung it to the other side of the room. She turned around quickly to grab another object, but as she turned around, she smacked her arm against the side of the table. She let out a scream of pain. It hurt so much! She sat down on her bed and looked at her arm. It was throbbing with pain. Her arm was bright red and she cradled it close to her body.

As she held her arm, Merlyn realised something she did not expect. Although she was in pain, she felt a little relieved. A small smile spread across her face. The sadness that she had been feeling all day was suddenly gone. Merlyn got up and picked up the lamp and book she had thrown. Then she got ready for bed.

The next day at school, Merlyn was sitting in class studying English. She was sitting beside her best friend, Bella. The teacher was telling the class to open page twenty of their English books. Merlyn was about to turn the page when a heavy sadness came over her. Before she knew it, she was fighting the urge to cry. There was no way she was going to cry in front of the whole class. That would be a nightmare!

Then Merlyn remembered how hitting her arm against her bedside table had helped make her sadness go away the night before. But she couldn't hit her arm. She had to try something else. Merlyn grabbed her right arm with her left hand. She dug her nails into her skin as hard as she could. It was working! Then she started scratching her arm around the same spot where she had dug her nails into. Her nails were sharp, and they were making her skin bright red. Her frustration and sadness were leaving her, and she didn't feel like crying anymore. 'Phew,' she thought, 'that was a close one. But I feel okay now.'

When Merlyn was in the kitchen that afternoon getting a glass of orange juice, she was wearing a t-shirt. Her mother was cutting vegetables at the sink. She glanced over at Merlyn and noticed the red marks on Merlyn's arm where she had dug her nails into in class. "What happened your arm, Merlyn?" she asked.

"Oh, this?" Merlyn said, looking at the mark. "I hit it off the door in school by accident."

"Okay, just be more careful next time," Merlyn's mother said.

"I will. I promise." That was a close one for Merlyn. But her mom believed her lie – or so she thought.

That night, Merlyn put her music on as loud as it could go and locked her bedroom door. She was alone, so no one would be able to hear her crying over the sound of the music. With her back against the wall, she slowly slid down it, collapsing on the cold floor. She started to cry, and once she had started, she couldn't stop. She felt so empty. Everything felt so hopeless.

Out of nowhere, Merlyn became angry. She jumped up and screamed. She picked up an ornament from her shelf and threw it against the wall. She paused and stared at her reflection in the mirror of her bedroom wall. She hated the person who was looking back at her. Screaming, she grabbed another ornament from the shelf and threw it at the mirror, smashing it into tiny pieces. Next, Merlyn started punching the wall as hard as she could. She punched it again and again, until her knuckles were red. She could see blood seeping through the cracked skin of her knuckles. It calmed her. It made her stop.

Merlyn went to the bathroom and ran warm water over her hand. She looked at her reflection in the mirror. Her eyes were still red from crying. "I hate you," she whispered to it.

She returned to her room, lay down on her bed and buried her head in her pillow, sobbing quietly to herself. She didn't leave the room until the next day.

"Merlyn, we're going to the movies! Get ready! If you hurry up, I'll even buy you popcorn!" Merlyn's mom called from downstairs.

"What are we going to see?" Merlyn yelled back.

"I think you'll like it, it's called Wonder Woman," her mother replied.

At the cinema, Merlyn watched in amazement as a female superhero flew around the world saving people from the gigantic, evil monsters who were trying to take it over. Wonder Woman was stronger than one hundred men combined. She used her powers for good and not evil.

"But mom, I thought that girls couldn't be superheroes? They're not big and strong like boys!" Merlyn said.

"Don't listen to anyone who ever says that," her mother replied, "Girls can be superheroes just as much as boys can. And Wonder Woman is here to remind you of that."

"Wow!" Merlyn gasped, still amazed at the movie she had just seen. "When I grow up, I want to be just like Wonder Woman! I want to save people from the monsters trying to take over the world, just like her!"

"You will," her mother said, beaming at her.

On the way home from the movies, Merlyn and her mother stopped at the shops for Merlyn to get a poster of Wonder Woman. The poster showed Wonder Woman fighting big, terrifying monsters, with burning buildings behind them. Merlyn loved Wonder Woman because Wonder Woman wasn't afraid of anything!

"Merlyn, listen to me now," her mother said. "Everyone has a monster living inside of them, but everyone has a superhero living inside of them too, to stop that monster. I know sometimes life can get hard, but those hard times help us to become much stronger than we were before the hard times. Every time you feel sad, remember these words, and it will remind you to be strong."

"I will. I promise," Merlyn replied.

The next night, Merlyn was sad and angry again for no reason and she didn't know what to do. She looked at her arm and thought about digging her nails into her skin or scratching her arm, so her pain and sadness would go away. She grabbed her arm and closed her eyes. She remembered the words her mother told her

– that she had a superhero living inside of her who would give her strength when she needed it most.

Merlyn opened her eyes and let go of her arm. She wasn't going to dig her nails into it. She looked up at the new poster of Wonder Woman that she had gotten just a couple of hours earlier. She gave it a confident smile. In that moment, Merlyn knew that she was strong enough to take on anything the world threw at her. She swore that she would never dig her nails into her skin or hurt herself in any other way, ever again. And she never did.

Bipolar Disorder

❖

Steve's Story

From the highest high to the lowest low,
In your most challenging times, your resilience will grow.

Steve was an ambitious young boy who worked hard at everything he did. He always liked challenging himself and getting better at anything he tried. He would always help his parents clean up after dinner and always did his homework as soon as he came home from school. He was happy at school and happy at home. He had no worries! One year, this all changed.

One day, Steve was lying in bed and didn't want to get up. This was unusual because he would normally be the first person to jump out of bed with a smile on his face every morning. When Steve's mom went into his room that morning to wake him up to get ready for school, Steve lied and said he had to stay in bed because he had a pain in his tummy. This was not like him to lie to his mother.

"What's wrong with me?" Steve sighed, "I don't want to get out of bed. I don't want to do anything today. What's the point in getting out of bed? I'm just going to stay here all day." When Steve did get up, he didn't talk to anyone, he just wanted to be on his own. He felt sad and empty for no reason. And he didn't like it at all.

At school, Steve didn't want to do anything. "What's wrong?" Michael asked him one day, "you don't seem like yourself."

"Nothing, I'm fine," Steve replied. But Steve wasn't fine. He wasn't fine at all. When all his friends were playing games at lunchtime, Steve wandered around the school on his own with his head down and his hands in his pockets. He couldn't pay attention in class. His head felt heavy. He felt lonely, even though he was surrounded by all of his friends.

At home, Steve wouldn't eat a single bite of dinner. He would grab a handful of biscuits and chocolate bars and go straight up to his room. He had no energy and didn't have any interest in playing his favourite games. Sometimes when he was in his room, he would cry for no reason. He didn't want to talk to anyone and only wanted to be on his own. He just watched movie after movie, alone in his bedroom, until it was time for bed. He felt sad like this for weeks.

One morning, Steve woke up and jumped out of bed. He felt so alive! "I'm the king of the world!" he shouted as he ran down the stairs as fast as he could.

"Steve, get back here immediately! You forgot to put on a t-shirt!" his mother cried as Steve headed towards the door.

"I don't care! I can do anything! I'm invincible! Whee!" Steve shouted as he ran outside into the garden and started running up and down in zigzag patterns, with his arms outstretched as if he were an aeroplane. He felt like he was unstoppable. He felt so alive! It was the best feeling in the world.

Later that week in school, Steve suddenly jumped out of his seat during class. "Let's go outside and play in the sun! Isn't outside beautiful?" he roared. "Why waste time in class when we can play outside!" and he ran out of the classroom.

"He seems happier," Bella said to Michael, "but the teacher will want to talk to him after school for that!"

When Steve was outside, he ran around the schoolyard laughing. He had never felt so happy.

That night, when it was time for bed, Steve wasn't tired and couldn't fall asleep. "I don't want to fall asleep, I'm not tired!" he moaned as he hopped out of his bed to play with his games. When he grew bored of playing with them, he started jumping on his bed! He laughed more and more with every jump. He stopped when his mother came into the room.

"Steve!" she roared, "it's three o'clock in the morning. Your father and I have work in the morning and you have school! Go to bed!" Steve tucked himself under his blanket and fell asleep. He slept for an hour and a half. When he woke up, he felt like he had gotten a whole night's rest! He was wide awake and decided to hop out of bed and play on his PlayStation until his alarm clock went off to remind him to get ready for school.

The next night, Steve was wide awake at two o'clock in the morning again. He took out his pencils, colours and sketchpad, and started drawing. He drew picture after picture. Two hours later he burst into his parents' bedroom.

"Mom! Dad! Look at the pictures I drew! What do you think?!" he shouted.

"Steve!" his father yelled. "It's four o'clock in the morning! Go to bed!"

But Steve didn't go back to bed - he played on his PlayStation again, and at seven o'clock he knocked on his parent's door to wake them up for work.

"Wake up! Wake up!" he yelled, banging the door. "It's morning time and it's time to get up!"

Steve ran down the stairs as fast as he could to have breakfast. He was still full of energy, even though he hadn't slept a wink the night before.

Steve went into school giddy and excited. In class, he put his hand up for every question the teacher asked. He spoke faster than usual and sometimes he even changed the topic of the question the class was discussing.

"Steve, we're learning about Maths right now!" his teacher cried, "We'll discuss your Irish homework later!"

Unfortunately, Steve didn't stay happy forever and he eventually became sad again. He stayed in his room all day and would cry for no reason again. Then one day, he felt happy and free again. He thought he could fly as he jumped through the air with excitement! He laughed at the smallest things and couldn't sit still.

Then he became sad again. His moods changed like this throughout the year.

Steve began to grow frustrated with the changes in his mood. When he was happy, he loved it! He wanted to stay like that forever. He felt like a superhero. He felt like he had superpowers and like he was the only person in the world who had them. His friends said that he was too happy and excited when he was like this around them. 'How can someone be too happy?' Steve wondered. But when Steve was sad, he felt the opposite. He didn't want to see any of his friends at all. He only wanted to stay in his room and be alone. "When I'm happy, my friends don't want to be around me, and when I'm sad, I don't want to be around them!" Steve sighed.

Growing concerned, Steve's parents brought him to see a doctor. They explained to the doctor that Steve's moods changed from extremely happy where he didn't want to sleep at all, to extremely sad where he just wanted to sleep all day. When he was happy, Steve would think he had superpowers. He would smile and laugh and run around all day and never get tired. When Steve was sad, however, he would mope around a lot and not talk to anyone. He wouldn't go out to play with his friends and he just wanted to be on his own.

"Hmm…" said the doctor, "It sounds to me like Steve may have bipolar disorder." The doctor turned to Steve and said, "Steve, sometimes people get happy and sometimes they get sad. However, your happy is much happier than their happy, and your sad is much sadder than their sad. It doesn't mean that this is a bad thing. It doesn't mean that there's something wrong with you. It just means that you're a little bit different, and I'm going to help you control your moods a little bit better than you are right now."

The doctor gave Steve an envelope and told him to open it whenever he felt a little lost in his life. That night, Steve was curious about the envelope that the doctor had given to him. He decided to open it to see what was inside. In it, there was a piece of paper that read: *From the highest high to the lowest low, in your most challenging times your resilience will grow.*

Steve wasn't entirely sure what that meant but with the help of his doctor and his parents, he knew that one day he would find out. He put the piece of paper away for safe-keeping until he needed it again. The doctor had said that life would become difficult again and Steve knew he would need to remember what was written on that piece of paper for when it did. He knew that he would be seeing a lot of his doctor over the next few months, but he was excited about learning more about bipolar disorder and the impact it could have on his life. Steve loved a challenge and bipolar was no different, and he was ready to show the world just how resilient he could be.

Anxiety

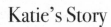

Katie's Story

*Her legs shake when she walks, her voice trembles when she talks.
Her heart beats so fast, how long will this pain last?*

Katie was a cheerful, caring girl, who would always look out for her family and friends. She dreamed of being the best football player in the world. "I'm going to win the World Cup for Ireland!" she would say. She was the captain of the school football team and loved to play the violin too. She enjoyed going to school and meeting up with her friends on weekends. One year, however, she began to feel different.

One day at school, the teacher asked the class a question. Katie knew the answer, but for some reason, she got nervous at the thought of answering it. Katie's heart began to beat really fast and her leg started to shake under the table. She put her head down so the teacher wouldn't notice her and wouldn't ask her a question. She was worried because she knew something was wrong, but she didn't know what. She had never been afraid to speak in front of the class before.

Little did she know that this was just the beginning.

The next morning when she was getting ready for school, Katie suddenly didn't want to go. She was worried something bad was going to happen to her parents. "Will you be okay? Are you sure you're going to be okay?" she kept asking them. She didn't want to leave them. On her way to school, Katie kept worrying that she would be asked a question in front of the whole class and she was worried that she wouldn't be able to answer it.

After a long day, Katie finally went to bed. But she couldn't sleep. 'What if there's a monster under my bed? Or looking in through my window?' she thought to herself. When she finally did fall asleep, she woke up again one hour later, and then two hours later for the second time. Her heart was beating really fast and it was hard for her to breathe. She was sweating all over and when she sat up, she was trembling! She felt confused and afraid and didn't understand why she felt this way.

In the morning, before going to school, Katie didn't tell her parents that she kept waking up during the night. She didn't want them to be worried. On her way to school, Katie was tired from not sleeping well. She was afraid that she would have to talk in front of everyone and that she would embarrass herself.

That day, the teacher gave the class a puzzle and told them to split up into groups to solve it. Katie was too shy to offer any ideas to her group. Her hands were sweating, and her heart was racing. When the teacher asked Katie's table for an answer and it was Katie's turn to speak, no words came out. The whole class started laughing. This was Katie's worst nightmare coming true! Katie jumped out of her seat and ran out of the classroom.

Katie ran to the bathrooms and started crying. She was so embarrassed! She didn't want to go back to the classroom and see everyone. 'I bet they're laughing at me right now. They're going to tell all of their friends. The whole school will know and make fun of me! They're going to call me the-girl-who-couldn't-talk forever!' she thought.

Katie didn't understand why she felt so afraid all of the time. Life used to be so different. All she wanted to do was to go home and never go back to school, ever again.

Over the next few weeks, Katie began to hide in her room and avoid her friends more and more. She was the captain of the girls' football team, but she stopped going to training. She loved playing music, but she stopped going to music practice. She told her parents that she didn't like football anymore and was going to stop playing. But that was a lie. She loved football! But every time before she was about to go to training, Katie's legs would get very heavy and she would get a feeling in her stomach like she was about to get sick. She felt like this before music practice too. She hated this feeling and decided to quit training and playing because of it.

As time went by, Katie began feeling more and more afraid. She was afraid to go on buses. They were filled with people, and too many people all in one place was scary. She was too shy to go down to the shop to buy a packet of her favourite sweets. The thought of talking to people she didn't know made her feel dizzy.

Katie's world had started to turn upside down. A once happy, outgoing girl was now a timid and uncomfortable one who couldn't even say hello to someone in public. Katie didn't want to see her friends, she didn't want to go anywhere she didn't have to. Every time she was with people, she felt nervous and shy. Her heart would beat faster and faster, her hands would shake. Sometimes she couldn't even get the words she wanted to say out of her mouth. Shaking hands was scary. Even hugging her own mam and dad was hard. She felt weak all of the time. She couldn't look anyone in the eye anymore – she would just look away.

Over the summer holidays, Katie locked herself in her room for days. She would only leave the room when it was time for dinner.

One day, Katie heard a knock on the door.

"Hi Katie, I'm Ana. I'm a friend of your mother's. Can I come in?"

"I guess," Katie replied, looking down at the floor.

"I heard that you're not feeling too good these days, is that true?" Ana asked.

"I guess so," said Katie, fidgeting in her seat.

"Can you tell me how you are feeling?" Ana asked.

Katie paused, reluctant to tell someone she didn't know how she was really feeling.

Seeing the uncomfortable expression on Katie's face, Ana said, "It's okay if you don't want to talk. You don't have to tell me anything you don't want to. But in my experience, when something happens that makes me upset, talking about it really helps me to understand the problem and makes me feel better."

For the first time since Ana had entered the room, Katie looked her in the eye. She was still shy, but something Ana had just said made her feel like she wasn't alone. For the first time since her troubles began, she felt she had finally found someone who could understand what she was going through.

"I feel nervous all the time," Katie said. Her voice trembled as she spoke, and her hands were shaking because she was scared to say any more.

Ana took Katie's hands in hers, which made Katie less frightened and gave her the courage to continue. "I feel scared when I think about seeing people. When I go outside I feel dizzy, my hands and legs start shaking. My heart races, it gets hard to breathe... I worry something bad will happen to my parents while I'm at school. I worry all the time about what other people think of me. I worry —"

"I'm going to stop you right there," Ana said. "It sounds like you have anxiety. You overthink things. You worry about things that may not even happen. And you worry about things that have already happened. That's a lot of things to be worrying about! No wonder you're not okay. If I worried as much as you do, I'd stay in my room all day too." With that, Ana reached into her bag and took out a rock, no bigger than her hand. She handed it to Katie.

"Does this feel heavy to you?" she asked.

"No," Katie said, holding the rock in both of her hands, "it's light."

Ana smiled. "People with anxiety overthink things, and by doing that, they make their problems seem much bigger than they really are. Right now, this rock you're holding in your hands isn't heavy and is easy to hold, isn't it? But if I were to tell you to hold on to it for a long time, not to let go of it, to take it with you everywhere you go, that small rock would eventually become harder and harder to hold, and would begin to seem much heavier than it really is," she explained.

"And, as you take that small rock with you everywhere you go, you'll start collecting even more rocks along the way. In your mind, just one of those small rocks will feel much bigger than it really is, so all of them together will be impossible to carry. Eventually, the rocks will become so hard to hold on to that they'll drop right out of your hands, and you'll fall down too because you'll have carried their weight for so long," Ana continued. "People with anxiety overthink things and worry too much and, just like that small rock becoming a big, heavy one the longer you hold onto it, your problems will seem much bigger than they really are too."

"Wow!" Katie gasped. "So how do I not make my problems become much bigger than they really are?"

"Sometimes you have to look at that small rock and say 'I don't need to carry you. You have no power over me!' and just let it go," Ana replied. "And when you let it go, all of your problems become that little bit smaller. Right now, you're stuck in the same spot because of everything that you're holding on to in life, but sometimes to move forward you have to leave some things behind. And when you learn how to let one thing go, you'll know how to let go of everything bad that comes your way in the future."

"But how do I let it go?" Katie asked, with a glimmer of hope in her eyes.

"That's what we're going to work on," Ana said with a smile.

Katie and Ana spent the next hour talking. Ana told Katie that in order to get over her fears, she had to look them in the eye and say, 'I'm not afraid of you.' She advised Katie to go back to playing football with the team she was once the captain of. She told her to drink lots of water, eat healthy food and get lots of sleep, because she needs to be at her strongest to face her fears. She told her to go out and see her friends again. But most importantly, she told her that sometimes life would be hard and scary, but that she would be strong enough to face it.

From that day on, Katie tried her very best not to worry and overthink things. It wasn't easy, some days she wanted to go back and stay in her room for the whole day, but she remembered what Ana had told her, that she was strong enough to face anything. She also remembered the story of the small rock and how holding on to it for longer than you should makes the rock seem much bigger than it truly is.

Katie went back to playing on her football team. She started to play music and enjoy school again. And most importantly, she was able to go outside and have fun again! She was able to spend time with her friends and even have conversations with strangers. It wasn't always easy for Katie, but she tried to let things go when she didn't need to hold on to them and that made all the difference.

Learning to let go of the things that were causing her problems, not worrying as much and not making her problems seem much bigger than they really were, helped Katie enjoy her life a lot more and helped her not to feel scared all the time. Katie finally understood that in order to beat her problems she had to stand up and fight them. And Katie was a fighter. She learned how to let go of the small rock she was carrying and helped others to let go of all the rocks they were holding on to, too. She worried less about the little things in life, and that helped her be a lot happier.

Depression

❖

The King Who Wouldn't Get Out of Bed

Sometimes the bravest thing you can do is to get out of bed
When all you can feel is the sadness in your head.

Once upon a time in a faraway land, there lived a king, his queen, their children and one hundred of the hardest-working servants in the world. The king had the biggest castle in all the land, and all the gold a king could ever ask for. On the outside, he appeared to be the luckiest man in the world. On the inside, however, he was miserable. And he wished that he wasn't the king.

One day, the king and queen were walking in their beautiful garden full of trees and rose bushes. The prince and princess were riding their horses. The sun was shining, the birds were singing and there wasn't a cloud in sight. It was a beautiful day. But to the king, something didn't feel quite right. As the king wandered the garden with the queen, he couldn't help but think about why he wasn't feeling good. 'I have a beautiful wife, beautiful kids, a big castle, lots of land and all the gold a king could ever ask for. So why am I so sad?' he wondered to himself, ignoring what the queen was saying beside him. This would be a question he would ask himself many times over the next few months.

Later that day, the king was having dinner in the great hall. The cooks had prepared a delicious meal for him, with two servings of dessert. "Two servings of dessert," the king sighed, "I'm eating a delicious meal, but I don't want any of it. I don't want to eat. I don't want to do anything. I don't want to see anyone. I just want to be alone. I'm going back to bed!" And that's just what he did.

One week later, the king was still in bed. He had not left his room all week. He only ate one meal a day. He wouldn't speak to anyone. He stopped washing himself. He didn't care about any of those things anymore. All he wanted to do was to stay in bed.

"I have all the things in life a king could ever ask for. So why do I feel as if I have nothing at all?" he asked himself. He was about to learn that there was something more important in life than having lots of money.

One day, the king was standing in front of the window and he started to throw many of his prized possessions out of it, shouting: "Take it! Take it all! It's all worthless. All this gold is supposed to make me happy but all it does is make me sad. I don't want it. Take it! Take it all, I say!" Everyone lucky enough to be standing below gleefully picked up the gold the king had decided to throw away. "Fools," the king muttered. "They will see that gold won't make them happy. There is no such thing as happiness. The world is and always will be full of pain and sorrow." With that, the king returned to bed and went back to sleep. He had not left his room in over two weeks.

As time passed by, the king's family grew more and more concerned about him. "We must get the king out of bed, he needs to serve the people," said the queen. "We need our king back." The prince and princess agreed. They would try to get him out of bed. The next day, the queen went into the king's room to try to get him out of bed.

"Why don't you get up?" the queen asked.

"What's the point?" the king replied.

"You need to get out of bed and serve the people as their king," the queen answered. "You could be the richest man in the whole world."

"There's not enough gold in the world to make me happy," the king sighed. "I'm not getting out of bed," and he turned over to go back to sleep.

The next day the prince and princess tried to get the king out of bed.

"Dad! Get up!" they said together.

"Why? What's the point?" answered the king, with one eye open.

"You have the biggest castle in the whole world," the prince said.

"And more land than anyone," the princess added.

"The only space I need is right here in this bed," the king sighed, "I'm not getting up." And he rolled over to go back to sleep.

The queen, prince and princess had all failed to get the king out of bed. "It's no use," said the queen, "I'm afraid he'll never get out of bed!" The prince and princess agreed. They didn't know what to do. "How can someone so rich be so unhappy?" asked the princess, "I thought being rich was the most important thing in the world."

But it wasn't.

As time passed, rumours started circulating around the castle about what the king now looked like. No one had seen him in two months. He had his own secret area in the castle where he stayed. Not even the queen stayed in the same room as him anymore.

"I heard his hair is so long it's down to the floor!" one of the castle servants said.

"I heard his fingernails are so long they're longer than his arms!" said another.

In truth, the rumours weren't completely wrong. The king hadn't washed in two months. His teeth were yellow because he no longer brushed them. His hair had grown down to his waist. He had a big, grey beard. He had lost a lot of weight. He was a shadow of the man he used to be. He stayed up at night staring into space and slept during the day. He was surrounded by darkness.

One day, when the king was in bed, one of the servants went into the room to bring him a bowl of soup. "I told you I'm not getting out of bed!" the king snapped.

"It's only me, Your Majesty. I'm just bringing you a bowl of soup," the servant said, with the bowl in his hands.

"I didn't ask for any soup. I don't want it!" said the king.

"I know, but I thought you might be hungry. Life is worse when you don't eat."

"Oh fine! Bring it over!" the king said as he took the bowl of soup. By the time the servant came back to collect the bowl, the king had finished it all. "That was delicious," he said.

"I'm glad you liked it," the servant said, with a smile. "Are you feeling any better?"

"Sometimes... sometimes I don't want to go to sleep so I don't have to wake up in the morning. I'm just so sad and I don't know why. I have a big castle, lots of land, and all the gold a king could ever need. I should be the happiest man in the world... But I'm not. I'm not happy at all. And I don't know why." After saying those words, the king felt as though a big weight had been lifted off his shoulders.

With a smile on his face, the servant replied, "Happiness does not come from having a big castle and lots of land. All the gold in the world won't matter at all if you can't learn how to laugh and be happy." With that said, the servant turned around to leave the king's room, but on his way out, he dropped the empty soup bowl.

"Here, let me help you!" said the king, jumping out of bed to help clean up the mess.

"Thank you, Your Majesty," the servant said, as he stood up.

"Wow!" the king exclaimed, "Suddenly, I don't feel as sad anymore!"

"Sometimes helping someone will make you much happier than being helped," the servant replied.

"Thank you," said the king, "I feel much better now. I'm going to get dressed and finally leave this room!" For the first time in months, the king felt hopeful that he could at last be happy again.

When the king left his room that day, he knew he had learned a valuable lesson. Big castles, lots of land and all the gold in the world won't make you happy on their own. There are more important things in life, like helping others and finding what you love to do and doing it. From that day on, the king was much nicer to all his servants and would help them out with their jobs in his spare time. He taught the prince and princess the importance of being kind to others. He would bring the queen a flower from the garden every day. He even gave each of his servants a piece of gold as a thank you for all their hard work.

One day, the king was walking outside in his garden. The clouds turned grey and it suddenly started to pour rain. Everyone else in the garden started running as fast as they could towards the castle to find shelter. The king put his hands out and looked up at the sky, letting the rain fall on him. He remembered the words of the servant, 'All the gold in the world won't matter at all if you can't learn how to laugh and be happy.' With that, the king laughed, and laughed, and laughed.

At last, he had learned how to be happy.

Anorexia

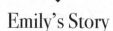

Emily's Story

*If it's happiness you seek, then one sure way to fail
Is signing your life away to the numbers on a scale.*

Emily was a confident young girl who gave her all to everything she did. She was the perfect student at school who got A's in all her tests and who her friends all admired. She also excelled at karate. One day she wanted to have a black belt! She was an only child who had a close bond with her parents. They always said that their daughter was the happiest girl in the world.

One day when Emily came home from school, she found her parents sitting at the kitchen table with serious looks on their faces. 'Uh oh. Have I done something?' she wondered. Emily's parents asked her to sit down and then told her the worst news she could have imagined – they were splitting up! Just like that, Emily's perfect world came crashing down and she didn't know what to do.

Emily went to her room to lie down on her bed. "Why is this happening?" she asked herself, "Is it because of me?" She looked in the mirror and said to herself, "Maybe if I looked nicer this wouldn't have happened. Maybe if I wasn't so fat my parents would still love each other. If I get skinny, then maybe they'll want to be together again!"

That day, Emily thought she knew what she had to do: she needed to lose weight. "All the girls in my school are so skinny and I'm so fat! It's not fair!" she cried. She looked in the mirror and didn't like the reflection that was staring back at her at all. "Why can't I be pretty like all the other girls? I bet everyone at school thinks I'm fat! I bet they all make fun of me when I'm not around. But I'm going to get skinny. They'll all see!"

The next day, Emily didn't have any breakfast. While she was having dinner, she secretly fed some of her food to her dog under the table. She put more bits of food into her pockets, and when she had to go to the bathroom, she flushed the food down the toilet. That night, she was so proud of herself. She went to bed hungry, but at least now, she thought, she was going to be skinny.

When Emily woke up the next day, she left the house before anyone else was awake. She started to run. She ran, and ran, and ran. She ran until she couldn't run anymore, and she fell on the ground, exhausted. When she got home, she only had a glass of water. "That was good," she said to herself. "I'll exercise again tonight."

As the weeks passed by, Emily's parents started to notice that she was going out running every day and not eating as much food as she used to. Emily had also started lying to them. This was not like her at all, she had never lied to them before! She would tell her parents that she had eaten before they got home from work or that she had had food at a friend's house. She exercised in secret, and she trained in the morning while her parents were still asleep, or at night when they were in bed. Emily even wore baggy clothes to hide how much weight she had lost. She had begun to live a secret life that only she knew about.

Emily tried to skip meals as often as she could, and some days she wouldn't eat anything at all. Every day, Emily would do one thousand sit-ups, one thousand star jumps, and she would run for two hours. When it rained and no one was home, she would run up and down the stairs until she couldn't stand anymore. Her parents were beginning to get worried over her obsessive behaviour. But she didn't care. In her mind, the only thing in the world that mattered was being skinny.

Emily spent a lot of her free time cutting out images of thin, beautiful women from magazines and putting them in a box she named the *Perfect Bodies* box. Every day, she would look at the pictures of all the women she had cut out and cry. "Why am I so fat?" she moaned. "Why can't I look like all these girls in the pictures? It's not fair!" Emily used the *Perfect Bodies* box as motivation to lose weight. Every day, she would add more photographs to the box. And every day, she trained harder and tried to eat less.

One night before she went to bed, Emily looked in the mirror and said to her reflection, "You are fat. But one day you won't be." She reached into her pencil case and took out a red marker and wrote 'YOU ARE FAT' on the mirror. For the next two weeks, she would look at those three three-letter words and push herself even harder to lose weight.

One day, Emily was out running on her favourite trail. It was a beautiful day. The sun was shining, the sky was blue, and there wasn't a cloud in sight. It was the hottest day of the year. She was wearing warm, baggy clothes to hide how much weight she had lost, and she hadn't even brought a drink of water with her for when she'd get thirsty. Emily ran and ran. She had been out in the sun for almost two hours and was starting to feel faint because of the heat.

"Stop!" her mind screamed at her.

"No!" Emily shouted back. She was exhausted. She had never been this tired before. The sun was making her feel dizzy. "I'm still not skinny enough! I need to be skinny! I... need... to be... skin..." With that, Emily collapsed. She had run for miles and couldn't go on any further. "Maybe I'll just take a little rest," she said, closing her eyes.

"Strange place to fall asleep!" Emily awoke to a soft voice. "Here, let me help you up." A slim, dark-haired woman with brown eyes and a warm smile stood over her.

"Where am I?" Emily asked, still weary from her run.

"You're on the walking track. My guess is that you're taking a break from running so hard. Here, have a drink," said the woman, handing her a bottle of water.

"Something like that," Emily muttered, taking a gulp of water.

"Why were you training so hard anyway?" asked the woman.

"I just... I just..." mumbled Emily, struggling to find the right words, "I just want to be skinny. Everyone at school is so skinny and I'm so fat. My parents are fighting with each other and splitting up, and it's all my fault!" Emily started to cry. And once she had started to cry, she couldn't stop! All of the feelings she had hidden from the world for so long were finally coming out.

"You're not fat, what are you talking about?" the woman said, "And your parents fighting with each other and splitting up isn't your fault. I'm sure that they both love you very, very much.'

"I am fat," Emily replied, still crying, "I have to eat less. I have to exercise more. I have to get skinny." Emily then told the dark-haired woman she had just met everything that had been going on in her life recently.

After listening to everything Emily had to say, the woman replied, "You know, I used to be just like you when I was a little girl. I would go the whole day without eating and would train every single day. I thought anything bad that ever happened to me or my family was all my fault."

"How did you change?" Emily asked.

"I learned to accept who I am. I learned how to love myself," the dark-haired woman replied. "In life there are some things you can change and some things you can't. Sometimes bad things will happen and there won't be anything you can do about it. Sometimes, people will call you names and be mean to you for no reason, and you won't be able to make them change their minds because that's just who they are. Focus on what you can change and not on what you can't. Learn to accept who you are and do what you want to do in life. Do what makes you happy and let everything else take care of itself. There is a strong girl inside of you, let her out and you will be able to take on the whole world."

Emily was amazed by the woman. No one had ever spoken to her like this before.

Emily and the dark-haired woman walked back to Emily's house, talking about everything going on in Emily's life all the way back.

"Before I go inside can you tell me your name?" Emily asked. "I would love to know the name of the woman who helped me so much today."

The woman smiled down at her. "Mira is my name. It was so nice to meet you. I wish you the best of luck with everything. And remember what I said about eating all your fruits and vegetables!"

"I will!" Emily said. "Thank you for everything!" and she ran back to her house.

That night, Emily ate all of her dinner. Her parents were shocked! She had finished her food so quickly. "Is there any more?" she asked. Her parents just laughed. Their little girl was back to her normal, happy, cheeky self.

That night, Emily looked in her bedroom mirror and saw her reflection smiling back at her. Emily got a wet tissue and rubbed out the words 'YOU ARE FAT', which she had written on the mirror weeks ago. She took out her red marker and wrote 'DO WHAT MAKES YOU HAPPY' instead. Every time she would look in the mirror from now on, she would be reminded to love her life and her body, instead of hating them. She would remember the words of Mira, who had taught her that there are some things in life you can control, and some things you can't. Emily didn't know what was going to happen in life, but somehow, she knew that it was all going to be okay.

Phobias

❖

Bruce's Story

Everybody gets afraid, everyone will get wary,
But when you stand up to the things you fear, all your fears will seem
less scary.

Bruce was a young boy who always boasted about how big and strong he was. "Feel my muscles, aren't they huge!" he would say to anyone who would listen. "One day, I'm going to be the biggest and strongest man in the whole world! And nothing can stop me because I'm not afraid of anything!" But there was one thing Bruce was afraid of, and he didn't want anyone to find out about it – he was afraid of dogs.

When Bruce was just five years old, he was at his cousin's birthday party. He was having so much fun with all his friends. The kids at the party played games and ate lots of cake and sweets. Bruce thought that it was the best day ever! When all the kids had finished eating, they went outside to play football in the garden where Wolfy the Labrador was. Wolfy got so excited when he saw everyone in the garden playing football that he wanted to join in! He ran up to Bruce to say hello and was so happy to see him that he jumped up on him and knocked him over. Bruce screamed with fear! He was terrified! Wolfy stood over him with his tail wagging and licked him before running off to chase the ball again. He wasn't trying to hurt Bruce, he was just being friendly and he forgot how big he was. However, from that day on Bruce was afraid of dogs.

Years later, Bruce's fear of dogs had only increased. He wouldn't go near one. But no one could ever know, he thought. Bruce's next-door neighbours had a dog called Buddy. Buddy was a big dog. He was a cross between a German Shepherd and a Labrador. His black and brown coating made him look even more frightening than he really was. He was a very big dog, but he was also the friendliest dog in the world.

Buddy was even bigger than Wolfy, Bruce's cousin's dog. As a result, Bruce was terrified of him and never wanted to see him. Bruce would always take the long route from his house to his school and the long way back, just so he could avoid him. Whenever he played football and the ball went into the neighbour's garden, he was too afraid to go up to their door and ask for it back. He was terrified because he thought Buddy would attack him.

One day, Bruce and his friend Eoin were walking back to Bruce's house after a long day of school. Bruce started taking the long way home. "Isn't it quicker to go this way?" Eoin asked, pointing to the road which was the short way to Bruce's house. Put on the spot, Bruce was forced to tell him about the big, scary dog called Buddy. "I have two dogs and they're friendly to everyone! I bet Buddy's friendly too," Eoin said.

Bruce told Eoin that when he was five, he was knocked over by his cousin's dog, Wolfy. He said that he knew it was silly to be afraid of dogs, but he couldn't help it. What if Buddy really wasn't friendly? Bruce made Eoin swear that he wouldn't tell anyone that he was afraid of dogs. "If people find out, they'll make fun of me!" he said.

"When I was younger I used to be afraid of water," Eoin said as they walked along the road.

"But why?" Bruce asked. "Water isn't scary!"

"I know," Eoin said, "but one day I saw a movie about sharks and I became afraid."

"How did you get over your fear?" Bruce asked, feeling a little relieved to know that he wasn't the only one who was afraid of something everyone else considered normal.

"I learned how to swim," Eoin said. "My mam took me to a swimming pool. Now I swim five days a week and I love it. Sometimes you have to face your fear to get over it. You have to take that leap of faith. In my case that was jumping into some water. Your leap of faith will be trusting that Buddy is not as scary as you think he is."

In that moment, Bruce knew what he had to do. "Let's take the short way," he said, and the two friends turned back to go the other way to see Buddy.

As Bruce and Eoin approached the garden where Buddy was, Bruce began to get nervous. His hands started to shake, his heart started to beat faster and faster, his legs felt like jelly!

"Who's a good boy?" Eoin said, patting Buddy on the head. "Come on over, Bruce. He's friendly!"

But fear got the best of Bruce and he started to run as fast as he could. Buddy started running too, thinking it was a game. "Stop running!" Eoin shouted, trying to catch up. But Bruce ran quicker and quicker, and, in his panic, he tripped over a stick and fell. As he was lying on the ground, Buddy stood over him and sniffed his face before running back to the house.

'Phew, that was a close one!' Bruce said to himself. When Bruce got home, he swore that he would never walk up to Buddy again. 'It's just not worth the risk — he's too dangerous!' he thought.

That evening when Eoin had gone home and Bruce was alone in his room, he heard a knock on the front door. He listened closely to find out who it was. He recognised the voice. He was shocked when he realized who it was. It was his neighbour. She must have seen him running away from Buddy.

"Bruce!" his mother called from downstairs. "The neighbours are going out for a while. They want to know if we'll mind their dog, Buddy, while they're gone. Why don't you come on down and say hello?"

'This is my second chance,' Bruce thought, as he started to walk down the stairs slowly. He was scared. He thought back to the time when Wolfy knocked him down at his cousin's party.

"He's friendly. Come over and say hello," his mother said, encouraging him to come over.

Bruce put out his hand, fearing the worst, but to his surprise, Buddy sniffed it and walked away. "Where's he going?" Bruce asked, but before his mother could give him an answer, Buddy came back with a toy.

"I think he wants to play," Bruce's mother said smiling. She knew Bruce was about to make a new friend. Bruce took the toy and brought Buddy outside to the garden.

Bruce spent the evening playing with Buddy. They ran around the garden, they played fetch, and when it got dark, they watched TV. When Buddy's owners came back to get him, Bruce didn't want him to go home!

"Please can he stay?" he begged.

"Come over to see him anytime," his neighbour said with a smile.

From that day on, Bruce was never afraid of dogs again. In fact, he loved them! Every day after school, Bruce took the short way home and stopped by to see his friend Buddy. He even got to bring him for walks on the weekends! The big scary dog that Bruce thought Buddy was, was really just a big friendly giant after all. "How could I have been so wrong?" Bruce asked himself. "I guess fear is only as big as you make it."

Over time, Bruce learned that the fear in his mind always made the things he was afraid of seem much more terrifying than they really were. Bruce even helped his friends get over all sorts of fears by teaching them that if you stand up and look your fears in the eye, you'll see that they're really not so scary after all. A spider doesn't want to hurt you, there is nothing about the dark to be afraid of, and if you can climb up a big tree, you can climb back down, no matter how high it is. And a dog, even a very big dog, just wants to be friends.

Schizophrenia

Bella's Story

She tells me how they make her feel when they tell me she's not real,
She's my friend that they can't see and she only speaks to me.

Bella was a bright, creative young girl who spent her free time in her room drawing and writing poetry. Bella loved the idea of being able to create something out of nothing. She would write poems and draw pictures of her friends, family and anything else that meant a lot to her. She dreamed of one day becoming a famous writer and artist. Whenever she wasn't in school or out with friends, she was in her room writing and drawing.

One day, Bella was outside in the garden sketching a picture of the birds in the trees.

"Bella?" said a voice.

Bella looked up. Standing over her was a girl who looked no older than her.

"Who are you?" Bella asked. "And what are you doing in my garden?"

"My name is Natalie," the girl said. "I have been searching for you for a long time."

"Why?" Bella replied, confused as to why a complete stranger was saying this to her.

"You don't belong in this world. You belong in my world where you are a powerful princess. It's a magical world where you have special powers. The prophecy says that when the princess returns, she will save her people and her land. Right now, the evil witch and her army have attacked and taken the kingdom. Every day, there are dark skies – the sun hasn't shone in years. You need to come home and save your kingdom. You need to defeat the witch and take on your rightful role as a princess."

Bella started laughing uncontrollably. This was the most ridiculous thing she had ever heard!

"Stop laughing! It's true!" Natalie insisted. "You're special. You're not like all the other people in this world. You will have magic powers and you will get them soon, when you come home with me to defeat the evil witch and save your kingdom. I have to go now but when I return, I will take you back with me, to your rightful home." Natalie then left. Bella couldn't believe what she had just heard. Surely it wasn't true! Was it?

As the days passed, Bella thought more and more about Natalie's visit and what she had said. What if what she had said was true? What if Bella belonged in a magical world where she was a princess? What if she had to go to her true home to defeat the evil witch? Bella had always felt like she was different, like she was a little magical, like she had secret powers and was born for a special reason. Maybe this was the reason.

One day, Bella was watching television when the channel suddenly changed on its own and started saying, "You must come home and defeat the evil witch!" over and over again. Bella turned off the television. She was shocked! "Did that just really happen?" she asked herself. "Maybe I just imagined it." She turned on the radio to listen to some music but, just like on television, she heard a message to her, repeated over and over. "Come home Bella," it said.

Feeling confused, Bella went outside for a walk to clear her head. She looked up at the sky. The clouds formed the shape of the words 'Come Home'. "Natalie was telling the truth!" Bella gasped. "All of these are signs! The television! The radio! The clouds in the sky! I have to go home to where I belong!"

That night, when Bella was about to go to bed, she heard a voice. It was a boy's voice. Bella looked around but there was no one there! "Listen to me Bella," the voice said. "I've been sent by Natalie. You are the princess of a magical world called Tír Dríochta and you must come home to defeat the witch. You are special. You are the most powerful princess in the world. You must be prepared to say goodbye to this world and get ready to come home to yours. You must not tell anyone about being a princess, or that you are leaving. They will only try to stop you."

From that night on, Bella heard the boy's voice in her head every day. It always said the same thing to her, that she was special and that one day she would have to leave to go to the magical world where she was a princess and where she would have to save the world from the evil witch. He also told her what to do and spoke to her when she was around other people, making it hard for her to concentrate when she was with them.

As well as the boy's voice, Bella also heard Natalie. She promised her that she would be back soon. She also heard the voice of a little girl who didn't speak much but when she did, it was to ask Bella when she was coming home. Although she could hear them, Bella couldn't see who the voices in her head belonged to, but they told her that she would see them when she finally returned to her true home, Tír Dríochta. Bella began spending less and less time with her friends from school and more and more time listening to the voices in her head.

Bella was ready to leave her home as she waited for Natalie's return. She had no way of even suspecting that something else was going on. It felt so real, she thought it was destiny. However, to the outside world it was clear that something strange was happening to Bella and her strange behaviour did not go unnoticed by her family and friends.

"Bella, would you like to come over to my house for a sleepover tonight?" Merlyn asked Bella one day at school.

"Say no," the voice in Bella's head hissed.

"I can't. My parents need my help to clean the house tonight. Maybe another time!" Bella said, as she ran off.

"That's odd," Merlyn said, turning to Michael. "I haven't seen Bella outside of school in weeks. She always says she's busy. I miss her. It feels like she has made new friends and doesn't want to talk to any of her friends from school anymore."

That night when Bella was in her room, she was called to come downstairs by her parents. They had grown concerned about how she was acting and wanted to talk to her. "Bella, is everything okay?" Bella's mother asked.

"We've noticed that you've been acting strange lately," her father said. "We've seen you talking to yourself outside in the garden. We've heard you talking to yourself in your bedroom."

"Don't tell them anything. Do not trust them," the boy's voice in Bella's head growled.

"Everything's fine," Bella said. "Can I go now?"

"You can, but we have decided to take you to a doctor tomorrow. Maybe you'll tell him more," Bella's mother said.

"No!" screamed the voice. "He'll find out!"

After hearing that, Bella shouted, "I'm not going! You can't make me!" and ran upstairs to her bedroom and slammed her door shut. What if they found out her secret? They would never let her go! She would never be a princess! She wouldn't be able to save her kingdom!

That night, Bella couldn't sleep. All she could think about was the magical world that was her real home.

"Hasn't anyone noticed that I'm not like everyone else?" Bella said, "I'm magical! I'm special!" But Bella was also confused. Maybe her parents were right? Maybe she was acting strange? Maybe she should tell somebody what was going on? As she lay in bed, all she wanted to do was to go to sleep, but the voices wouldn't let her. They kept talking to her all night.

"Hi Bella, how are you?" said the doctor the next day. "Your parents have filled me in on everything that's been going on lately. It can't be easy for you."

"Don't answer him," the boy's voice hissed.

But Bella had had enough. She needed to tell someone about what was going on. Maybe he could go with her and help her defeat the evil witch?

"Shut up!" Bella said in frustration to the voice in her head, as she looked away from the doctor. "I'm going to tell him, maybe he can help us."

"Who are you talking to?" the doctor asked, looking concerned. With that, Bella started crying and told him everything.

After listening to everything Bella had to say, the doctor said, "Bella, you love to draw and write poetry. You have an extremely creative brain. But it sounds like your brain has become a little too creative and it's making you see and hear things that aren't really there."

"Am I crazy? What is happening to me?" Bella asked.

"You're not crazy," said the doctor. "Trust me when I say this to you, you're not the first person I've met in this situation and you certainly won't be the last. I'm going to help you get better. Everything is going to be okay."

One year later, Bella was a very happy girl. She enjoyed school and would spend her weekends at the cinema or at the park with her friends. She still wrote and drew pictures every day. She still dreamed of writing a book and illustrating it one day. Every week, she went to her doctor, who helped her out whenever life became difficult or complicated. She hadn't seen Natalie or heard any voices in her head for a year. She didn't hear the television or radio speaking to her and she didn't see any signs in the sky. The magical land where she was a princess and had to fight the evil witch didn't exist.

One day, Bella was outside in her garden, sketching. "Bella, I'm back," a familiar voice said.

Bella looked up, she already knew who it was. "I've come back for you to bring you home," Natalie said.

"My doctor says I have a creative brain. Sometimes it gets so creative it makes me see or hear things that aren't real," Bella said.

"What are you trying to say?" Natalie asked, with a worried look on her face.

"What I'm saying is..." Bella paused for a second. This was a big moment for her. "You're not real. You're something my mind has made up. You exist in my head but not in the real world. I'm not going anywhere with you."

"They're lying to you just like I said they would!" Natalie said, "Your kingdom needs you! Come home with me!"

Bella stood up. "I believed you once," she said, looking at Natalie. "My doctor told me that one day I might see you again, and he said that if I did, I would have to be brave and tell you..."

"Tell me what?" Natalie asked, upset about what she was hearing.

"Tell you that I know you're not real. I'm not a princess. There is no evil witch or magical world. None of that exists. I'm not going to talk to you again, even if I see you. I won't listen to the voices in my head either. And when I do see you, I have to let my doctor know and then he's going to help me to not see you again.

He said that when life gets hard my mind creates things that aren't real, so I can forget about the things that are making my life so hard. But I'm not going to run away from the real world anymore. And to do that I have to say goodbye to you. I have to forget about the magical world that you say you come from." With those words said, Bella turned away from Natalie and started walking towards her house.

"Bella! Come back! I need you! Your world needs you!" Natalie cried, who was now panicking.

"Goodbye Natalie," Bella said, as she opened the door to her house. Bella looked up at the sky. The clouds had formed the words 'Come back Bella'. But Bella ignored them and walked straight into her kitchen.

Saying goodbye to Natalie was one of the hardest things Bella ever had to do. She knew that if Natalie had come back, then the voices in her head would be back soon, too. She knew that she would see messages in the sky and hear the television and radio talking to her. She knew that she couldn't ignore what had just happened in her garden and that she would have to call her doctor right away to tell him that Natalie had come back. He would help her.

Being able to say the words 'You're not real' to Natalie gave Bella hope that she would be strong enough to handle whatever her creative brain decided to throw at her in the future. It gave her hope that it was all going to be okay. And it was.

Addiction

❖

Peter's Story

Sometimes the things you want the most are the things you need the least.

Peter was a young boy who lived with his mom, dad and little sister, Chloe. To the outside world, he was the happiest boy in the world. But the truth was that he was miserable because of life at home. His family were poor, and they couldn't afford to have a dinner every day. They lived in a house that was so cold that Peter would go to bed wearing a jumper, and sometimes he would wake up in the middle of the night shivering. His parents fought all the time and Peter barely got to see them. All he ever wanted was a normal family life.

One day, Peter's mom came home and walked into the kitchen. Seeing the mess in the room, she asked,

"Why isn't the kitchen clean? Where's your father?"

"Daddy spent the money watching horses again," Chloe said, who was playing with her dolls at the table.

"Mom, are we having dinner tonight? We haven't eaten all day and I'm starving," Peter moaned.

"Of course, I'll see what we have," his mother said, taking bread out of the bread bin. "Here, make yourself a sandwich."

"But Mom, we had Nutella sandwiches for dinner last night," Peter whined. His stomach rumbled as he spoke. They hadn't had a hot dinner in three days.

"Well, I'm afraid that's all we have for now. Make a sandwich for your sister too. I'm going out to find your father."

"Why are mom and dad always fighting?" Chloe asked Peter, when it was just the two of them in the kitchen.

"They're just not getting on right now," Peter mumbled. "Now eat your sandwich."

At two o'clock in the morning, Peter was still wide awake in bed. He was quietly sobbing. He didn't know how much longer he could take the situation at home. He hated it. He had to be brave and strong for his little sister. Chloe was only six and didn't understand how bad things at home really were. Someone needed to tell her that everything was going to be okay. Peter's mother was trying her best to keep the family together. Peter knew that, he knew she was tired because of how hard she was working. She worked two jobs ever since his dad had quit his. But because of this, Peter barely got to see her, which he hated. He missed not seeing his mom every day.

Peter barely got to see his dad, either. Even though his dad didn't have a job, he would spend his days in the bedroom or in the kitchen on his laptop, checking the football scores or watching horse-racing. Peter always wondered why his dad loved them so much. When his dad's team or horse won, he would run around the house, jumping around celebrating. He would even break into song and dance from time to time! But when his dad's team or horse lost, he would blame everyone and anything in sight and go to the pub to drown his sorrows. One day, Peter's dad blamed Peter for his horse losing, because Peter had come into the kitchen to pour himself a glass of juice. Peter's dad shouted at him and told him he didn't want to see him again for the rest of the day. No one was allowed to come into the kitchen and disturb him while the horse-racing was on because it was bad luck, his dad said.

Peter hated his life. He was always hungry because his parents couldn't afford food and the house was always cold because they couldn't afford heating. When everyone was home, his parents fought all the time. Peter just wanted a normal, happy family like everyone else had. Was that too much to ask? Why was his family so different? He eventually stopped crying after thinking about these things and fell asleep.

The next afternoon, Peter was watching television in the living room when he was interrupted by loud screams from the kitchen.

"Get in! You beauty!" The living room door burst open and in danced his dad – the happiest that Peter had ever seen him. "Chloe, get in here! Kids, don't make any plans for next week, because I'm taking you to Disneyland!" The kids jumped up and down screaming with excitement! Was this really happening?

Just then, Peter's mother came in. "What's all the excitement about?" she asked, watching everyone hop around with joy.

"Baby, everything's going to be okay. Let's go out to a fancy restaurant tonight, wear your best dress. Those diamond earrings you wanted last Christmas but I couldn't afford, they're yours! Our troubles are over, believe me," their dad said, giving their mom a big hug and a kiss. There hadn't been this level of excitement in the house for a very, very long time.

"No! No! No!" shouted a loud voice from the kitchen the next day, and Peter had a horrible feeling that he already knew what it was. He ran into the kitchen to see what the problem was and found his father, red-faced, sitting at the table in front of his laptop.

"Dad, what is it?" Peter asked, anxiously.

"Nothing I can't fix, son," his dad replied, as he walked out the door to go to the pub. No doubt he would return home late that night, waking everyone up by slamming doors, knocking things over, and shouting and cursing, just like every other time his dad went to the pub to drown his sorrows. The next morning, Peter would always find his dad asleep on the couch, in filthy clothes and smelling of alcohol.

Over the next few days, Peter's mom and dad barely talked. They wouldn't even stay in the same room. It became clear to Peter that they would not be going to Disneyland and his mother would not be getting the diamond earrings his father had promised her just a few days earlier. But that was the least of their problems.

School was no fun for Peter or his sister. Sometimes they didn't have a school lunch because the family didn't have enough money. Both Peter and his sister wore old school uniforms that were tatty and too small for them. Peter enjoyed seeing his friends at school, but he couldn't help but feel jealous of them because they had a school lunch every day and brand-new school uniforms that fit them perfectly.

One day after school, Peter's dad came to collect Peter and Chloe from school.

"Would you like a bar of chocolate?" he asked them.

"Yes please!" they said together. It was rare that their dad bought them anything.

"Great. But you have to promise not to tell your mother, she won't like it if we tell her that you had chocolate before dinner!"

"We won't!" they promised.

"I have to go out for around twenty minutes, I'll be back then. Just stay here in the car and eat your chocolate and do your homework. Don't leave the car. And don't tell your mother I stopped at the shop before bringing you home. She'll only worry again for no reason. You know what she's like," Peter's dad said, as he got out of the car and walked down the street and out of sight.

Peter and Chloe sat in the car, happily eating their chocolate and talking about their day in school. Soon, an hour had passed and there was no sign of their dad. Twenty more minutes passed, and their dad still hadn't come back.

"Should we go out and look for him?" Chloe asked, confused to why he hadn't returned at the time he said he would.

"No, he said to stay here," Peter replied.

Two hours passed since Peter's dad had left them in the car on their own. They were starving, and the car was starting to feel chilly. "How much longer do we have to wait? I'm hungry and cold," Chloe moaned.

Chloe kept looking out the window, waiting for their dad to appear in the distance, while Peter continued to check the time on the red plastic watch he had gotten with a Happy Meal from McDonalds on his birthday less than a year ago. He was growing impatient, and Chloe's complaints were getting louder. "Let's go and find Mam," he said. "She's at work so we can't see her for long. But maybe she'll know where Dad is."

The kids got out of the car to go and see their mother at work. When they told her that their dad had left them in the car for over two hours, she couldn't hide her anger. "Wait here a minute, then we'll go to get some food and go home," she said.

When they arrived home that night, Peter's mother told the kids to go and watch television in the sitting room while she talked to their father in the kitchen.

"How could you?! You left them in the car on their own for hours!" Peter heard his mother scream at the top of her lungs.

"I know, and I'm so sorry. But look! One hundred euro! I won!" Peter's dad replied.

"I don't care how much money you won! You'll only lose it again tomorrow. We're done! No more! It's betting or your family. Choose!" The kids could hear their mother screaming all the way from the kitchen. They had never heard her this angry before.

"Just give me a few more days. I promise! I'll win it all back! We can have the future we've always dreamed of," Peter's dad begged.

"Pack your bags and get out! And don't come back until you can promise that you're not going to bet again!" Peter's mother yelled.

Just like that, the conversation was over and the kids heard the kitchen door slam shut. That night, Peter's dad went into each of his children's bedrooms to tell them he was going away for a while, but that they would see him again soon. He told them that he was sorry for everything but that he loved them very much. Peter and Chloe both cried themselves to sleep that night. They loved their dad and didn't want him to go away.

Three weeks passed. Peter hadn't seen his dad since the night his mom and dad had their big fight. His mom was forced to quit her job so that she could take care of the house and the kids. Peter could see that she was both tired and sad, but she never talked about it. Life wasn't easy, but Peter's mother told them that one day everything was going to be okay. They just had to have a little bit of faith.

One day, just over a month after he had left the house, Peter's dad came back! "Dad!" the kids screamed together, as they ran over to him to give him a big hug. Peter's mom just smiled and said, "You look better."

"I feel better," Peter's dad replied.

"I learned a lot when I was away, and while I still need some help, I'm much stronger than I was before. I'm so sorry for everything I put you and the kids through. It will be much different from now on. I promise."

"I believe you," Peter's mom said, smiling, as she walked over to give her husband a hug.

Two months later, Peter had the family life he had always dreamed of. His dad seemed much happier and had even found himself a job. Peter's mom went back to work too, but she didn't work long hours like before, so she still had the evenings to spend with her kids. Every day when Peter came home from school, there was a hot dinner on the table, and every night, he spent time with his family, laughing and joking, like he had always wished he could. Every night, the heating was on in the house and Peter even got the new school jumper he so desperately needed.

One morning, Peter's dad called him and his sister into the living room and told them news that would make their whole year. "Kids, we're going to Disneyland! We're going in two weeks. So try and hold in your excitement until then. I can't wait to go with you all. And I'm very happy with how life is going for us as a family. I wouldn't change it for anything. And if I can only ever teach you one thing in life, it's this: there is nothing more important than family. Always remember that."

And Peter always would.

Attention Deficit Hyperactivity Disorder (ADHD)

❖

Jessie's Story

Imagine a world, oh wouldn't you cry?
If you only judged a lion on how high he could fly.

Jessie was an intelligent young girl who had lots of energy and was always running around. Although Jessie was very clever, she found spending long periods of time sitting down reading books boring, and just wanted to be outside playing instead. Jessie swam, ran and played tennis. Tennis was her favourite, and she dreamed of one day playing at Wimbledon.

One day, Jessie was sitting in class reading a book. The class were taking turns to read out loud and it was going to be Jessie's turn to read soon. She needed to concentrate so she would know what line to read when it was her turn. But Jessie wasn't concentrating. Instead, she was looking out of the window at a squirrel in a tree. She didn't have a clue which page, never mind which paragraph, the class was on. This wasn't the first time Jessie hadn't been paying attention in class – whenever the class were doing something, she always found something else to focus on, like looking out the door or the window.

As well as losing concentration, Jessie always found herelf daydreaming, even when she didn't mean to. One minute, she could be listening to the class discussing a Maths question, and the next minute she could be in her own little world, where she would travel back in time to see dinosaurs or go to space and talk to aliens. Jessie enjoyed her daydreams. But she didn't enjoy being snapped out of one of them by the teacher in front of a giggling class.

Jessie also found sitting still in her chair very hard indeed. She would always shake her legs under her table, click or chew her pen or play with her hair while the teacher was talking. She always had a lot of energy, so sitting still was no easy task for her.

"Jessie? Jessie!" the teacher said.

"Huh?" Jessie said, looking up at her teacher.

"Jessie, if I asked you to read next, would you know where to read from? No. I would like you to move up to the top of the class, so I can keep a closer eye on you and make sure that you're paying attention. Maybe then you'll take school a little more seriously."

Jessie grabbed her books and her bag and swapped desks with the boy who was sitting at the front of the class. 'It's not fair,' she thought, 'everyone thinks that I'm not paying attention on purpose, but I swear that I'm trying!'

The next day at school, Jessie's class had an English test. Jessie was excellent at English and she was very confident that she would do well. When she got the paper, there were ten questions she had to answer in half an hour. When the exam started, Jessie answered the first three questions straight away. It was going so well! Then, however, she got bored and decided to take a short break from her test. She started to draw a picture at the side of her paper instead of answering the questions.

"Ten more minutes!" the teacher called to the class.

'Oh no!' Jessie thought to herself, 'I've spent most of my time drawing instead of doing the test!' Jessie rushed through the rest of her exam but only got as far as question seven before running out of time. When she received her test back from the teacher later that day, she saw that she got six out of ten questions correct, which was a C. Jessie had only answered six questions and had answered them all correctly, but because she had spent so much time drawing a picture, she hadn't had time to finish her test and ended up getting one of the lowest marks in the class. Jessie was extremely annoyed at herself when she got home that day for not doing better on the test. 'Everyone thinks I'm stupid, but I'm not! If I had just answered all of the questions, I would have gotten a much better score!' she moaned.

One day when Jessie was at home, she saw an advertisement for cycling on TV and decided that she would like to do it. "Mom, can I please get a bike, so I can join the cycling club?" she begged.

"No, you play three sports already!" her mom replied.

"But I don't like swimming anymore! It's boring!" Jessie whined.

It wasn't unusual for Jessie to get bored with the sports she did. She always grew tired of the things she did, and got extremely excited at the thought of trying something new. Her mother knew that she'd join a cycling club and most likely get tired of it soon after and then want to take up something new again, maybe gymnastics, ballet or even horse riding.

Jessie's hobbies weren't the only things she would get bored of. She loved to make puzzles and jigsaws, but she always found them difficult to complete because her attention always switched to something else. She would always get extremely excited about trying something new but once she was doing it, she would lose interest and find something else that grabbed her attention. Even when Jessie was doing her homework, she would switch from English to Irish to Maths to Science without finishing one subject completely first.

When Jessie's parents asked her to do some housework, Jessie would get bored and take big long breaks, which meant it took a lot longer for her to finish her jobs around the house than it should have.

On one fine sunny day at school, Jessie and the rest of the girls in her class were sitting under the trees, getting shade from the sun. The boys were playing football in front of them. All the girls were deep in conversation with each other except for Jessie, who was in a world of her own. 'Look at all the birds flying in the sky. They're up so high! Imagine if people could fly like birds. I would fly all day. I would fly away from here and...'

"Jessie?" a girl from Jessie's class called Jasmine said, interrupting Jessie from her thoughts.

"What?" Jessie replied, snapping out of her daydream.

"What did you think of the Maths test today?" Jasmine asked. This was her third time asking Jessie this question, but Jessie had been daydreaming and didn't hear her asking it.

"Oh sorry, I didn't hear you. I thought it went okay." Jessie said, bored of sitting down and eager to have some fun. As the football the boys were playing with landed near the girls, Jessie jumped up and grabbed it.

"Hey! Give that back!" the boys yelled, as Jessie ran away laughing.

Jessie ran back to the girls sitting in the shade and got them to join in with her, as they passed the ball to each other, keeping it away from the boys for as long as they could.

"Jessie, sometimes you have way too much energy!" Jasmine joked after the bell rang as they were walking back to class.

Jessie's wandering mind was beginning to cause problems for her both at home and at school. At home, her parents were growing frustrated with her for forgetting to do housework that she always promised to do. On top of that, Jessie's bedroom was a mess. There were clothes all over the floor and sometimes her room would get so messy that Jessie would have to walk over her toys and clothes just to get to her bed! She would always promise herself that she would tidy her room later, but whenever she started cleaning it, she would get bored after ten minutes and lie down on her bed or just leave her room to do something else.

At school, Jessie still found it hard to pay attention, even though she had moved to the front of the class. She still daydreamed, was restless in her chair, and looked anywhere but down at her books. Because of this, she often missed out on what the class was doing and the quality of her homework and grades were suffering. She began to start feeling very bad about herself, and she didn't know what to do.

One day, Jessie's parents decided to meet with her teacher to talk about her low grades at school. Jessie's teacher told them that Jessie was having trouble paying attention in class and that she was concerned because she could see that Jessie was a very bright, young girl. She also told them that she used to teach another little girl who had had trouble sitting still in her chair and concentrating in class, just like Jessie. As a result, that little girl's schoolwork had suffered. She said that after seeing a doctor, the little girl found out that she had something called Attention Deficit Hyperactivity Disorder or, ADHD. The teacher advised Jessie's parents to speak to a doctor to find out more.

After talking to a doctor, who agreed that it sounded like Jessie had ADHD, Jessie's parents and teacher worked together to make sure Jessie could do her best at school. Jessie confessed to her parents that she had begun to feel very bad about herself and was worried that she just wasn't good enough at anything. She even said that she was starting to think that she wasn't as smart as the other kids in her class, but Jessie's mother told her, "You are good enough. You are not stupid. Some people just learn and think in different ways to other people. If you judge a lion by his ability to fly, he will never know that he's the king of the jungle. You're a very smart and talented young girl. Soon, you will see this for yourself." After hearing this from her mother, Jessie felt better.

Over time, with help from her doctor, her parents and her teacher, Jessie learned how to pay more attention in class. The quality of her homework improved and instead of Cs, Jessie got As. At home, she was able to do the housework on time and learned how to focus for longer on the things she was doing, like drawing a picture or making a jigsaw. She was very happy that she was seeing a doctor for her ADHD, and life at home and school was much better now because of it.

Jessie learned that no one was stupid, and that some people just have different ways of learning. She had found out how to learn to the best of her ability, and as a result was getting the best grades in her class. She was excelling outside of school too. She would never have known how gifted she was if she hadn't gotten help. Jessie was the happiest she had ever been - she was more confident than ever, and she was extremely excited to see what life had in store for her, now that she had a better understanding of her mind.

Bigorexia

Ryan's Story

Big muscles can only carry you so far.

Ryan was a cheeky, energetic young boy who always liked having a joke and a laugh. He loved to play sports, with running and rugby being his favourite. Although he was the smallest player on his rugby team, he was the fastest, and what he lacked in strength and size, he made up for in speed. Ryan proved that size was not everything if you wanted to be good at sports.

One day at school, the boys were playing rugby outside in the sun. Ryan, who was the best player in the class, scored try after try as he ran past the other boys. The bigger boys in the class, feeling embarrassed that they couldn't catch Ryan, decided the only way to beat him was to play rough. They began to bully him by pulling his shirt, tripping him up and pushing him over. "You're so small and skinny!" one of the bigger boys taunted. "You'll never be big and strong like us!" When the bell rang to go back to class, Ryan felt relieved that the game was over.

That day when Ryan came home from school, he was very upset over what had happened when he was playing rugby. He looked at his arms in the bathroom mirror and hated what he saw. "I'm so skinny! Why can't I be big like all the other boys?" he moaned.

Ryan began to grow more and more insecure with the way he looked. He hated the sight of his small, skinny body and wished he could have bigger muscles. When Ryan was in the changing rooms at rugby training, he was too frightened to take off his t-shirt in front of the other boys in case they would think he was small, skinny and weak, and call him names. He couldn't even look at his body in the mirror at home because he was so unhappy with the way he looked. He even started to shower with his t-shirt on because he was so ashamed of it!

One weekend, Ryan was so sad because of the way he looked that he didn't leave his house. He just stayed in his room watching movies. He watched action movie after action movie. As he watched each movie, he noticed that the lead characters in all of them had one thing in common – they were all huge! That weekend, Ryan came to believe that if you were a boy, the only thing that really mattered in life was to be big and strong.

That night, before going to bed, Ryan did ten push-ups and ten sit-ups. "It's not much, but one day I'll be able to do a thousand of each!" he said to himself. Ryan looked at his muscles in his bedroom mirror. They already looked and felt a bit bigger. He smiled to himself as he flexed in front of the mirror, imagining to himself that one day he would be the man with the biggest muscles in the whole world.

The next day, Ryan did ten push-ups and ten sit-ups first thing in the morning and he did the same thing again last thing at night. Soon, ten push-ups and ten sit-ups became too easy for him and he increased it to twenty of each exercise every morning and night. Ryan noticed that his muscles had grown, and every time he passed a mirror, he couldn't help but stop to flex his arms. He was delighted with how much bigger and stronger he had already become.

At his twelfth birthday party, Ryan ate two slices of cake and a whole bag of sweets. When he looked in the mirror the next day, he was ashamed of the way he looked. He felt dirty and fat! He was angry with himself for eating so much unhealthy food. He did thirty push-ups and thirty sit-ups that night to make up for everything he had eaten at the party.

The next day, Ryan went to the shop to buy some fitness magazines. Every magazine he saw had a big, muscular man on the front cover. "Wow!" he gasped, "How will I ever look like these guys? I need to train even harder!" He bought ten magazines to bring home with him that day to read so he could learn more about growing big and strong.

As time went on, Ryan trained harder and harder. He managed to get a chin-up bar in his room and he bought his first ever set of weights in his local sports shop. Ryan trained for an hour every morning and every night, every day of the week, without ever taking a break. He would do push-ups, sit-ups, squats, chin-ups, shoulder presses, lunges, triceps dips, and more. He would do ten of each exercise in a circuit. When he finished doing every exercise in the circuit, he would take a quick water break before doing the circuit all over again. He would do the circuit at least five times per workout.

Working out wasn't the only thing Ryan was doing to get bigger – he ate everything in sight, so he could grow bigger muscles. Every morning, he would have a bowl of porridge with two full eggs, four egg whites and a glass of orange juice. He tried to stuff the food down his throat as fast as he possibly could, so he would have his breakfast finished before leaving for school. Sometimes, he would eat so much food that he would get sick before he left. He would often have a sandwich after dinner just to eat more. Ryan wanted to be as big and strong as possible, and for that to happen, he had to eat a lot of food. On days where he didn't eat as much as he would have liked, he would hate himself and feel guilty.

One night, Ryan was getting ready for bed. He was exhausted from training so hard without having a day off. His body was sore and tired from working out and all he wanted to do was to go to bed. "One night without training couldn't hurt, could it?" he asked himself.

He was about to see what would happen when he missed a workout.

That night, Ryan couldn't sleep. He kept worrying what would happen, now that he hadn't trained before going to bed. 'When you wake up, you'll be skinny again. You will have lost all of your muscle. You will be small and weak again and everyone will make fun of you. And you could have stopped this, but you didn't train because you're weak. And it will be all your fault,' Ryan's mind kept telling him. As the minutes went by, each minute seeming longer than the last, Ryan worried more and more that he would wake up skinny again, all because he hadn't trained.

Ryan couldn't take it anymore! He decided to make a deal with himself. He would get up and do one thousand sit ups on the condition that he could then stop worrying and finally go to sleep. He calmed down a little bit once he made this deal. He got out of the bed and sat down on the floor, ready to start training.

He counted: "1, 2, 3... 100! Keep going Ryan, still a long way to go... 101, 102... 500! Halfway there. Don't you even think about getting tired... 501, 502... 900! Well done, keep it up. Don't be weak and give up now... 901, 902... 1000! Finally! Now go back to bed." When Ryan looked at the time on his clock, it was after two in the morning! He needed to go to sleep so he could get up for school the next day.

Over the next few months, all the boys on Ryan's rugby team and in his class started noticing how much bigger his arms were getting, and it wasn't long before they were asking him for workout advice. Ryan liked the fact that people didn't think he was small and weak anymore but when he was alone, he still trained harder than ever. He still didn't like how his body looked when he looked at it in the mirror. He still didn't feel like he was big enough.

Ryan was exhausted from training twice a day, every day, and he hated the fact that he ate so much food that it made him throw up. If he was sick and couldn't train, he panicked about losing all the muscle he had worked so hard for. He wouldn't even leave the house if he went a day without training because he felt skinny and was disgusted with himself.

One day, Ryan was working out in his room when his dad walked in.

"You're still training? How many chin-ups can you do now?" his dad asked, as he grabbed the chin-up bar and did twenty chin-ups.

Determined to beat his father, Ryan grabbed the bar and started doing chin-ups.

"One, two, three, four, five, six, seven, eight, n ..." his dad counted. "Eight! Not bad, son, well done!"

Ryan got angry and punched the wall. "It sucks!" he shouted. "I'm weak! I'm not strong like you."

"Why are you angry? Eight is great for someone your age!" Ryan's dad said, with a concerned look on his face.

"No, it's not. It's awful. I bet you're ashamed of me..." Ryan said, with his head bowed down in shame.

"Why would you think that?"

"Because I'm not big and strong like you! And the most important thing in the world if you're a boy is to be big and strong." Ryan put his hands in his pocket and avoided eye contact with his dad. He was embarrassed because he wasn't able to do as many chin ups as him and was afraid that his dad thought he was a loser because of it.

Ryan's dad was confused to why his son was upset and motioned him over to sit on the bed beside him. "Ryan, let me tell you something that every young boy your age should know. Being big and strong is not the most important thing you can be as a man. What you do in life, how you treat others and how you act in your most difficult moments are much more important than having big, huge arms."

That day, Ryan told his dad how much he trained and ate every day and why. All he wanted to do was to be big and strong and not be small and skinny anymore. He was shocked to learn that, just like him, his dad also used to train really hard when he was Ryan's age because he was also afraid of being small and skinny. Ryan always thought his dad was invincible and not scared of anything! And now he knew that his dad used to be anxious about his appearance just like him once upon a time.

Ryan learned that while training is a good thing, overtraining can be bad for you. He learned that the body needs time to recover and rest after a workout, and that training the same muscles every day does more harm than good. He learned that if he really wanted to get bigger and stronger, he would need to learn how to train correctly and safely. He learned that he had to have a balanced diet and not just throw as much food as possible into his mouth, any chance he got. But most importantly, Ryan's dad told him that training was for fun! After all, what's the point in training if you're not going to enjoy it?

In time, Ryan learned how to be happy in the body he had. He didn't train nearly as much as he used to and had much more energy because of it. He no longer ate so much food that he felt sick or puked. He was able to take days off training without feeling guilty. He stopped comparing his body to actors' bodies in action movies. But most importantly, Ryan learned that there are more important things in life than having the biggest muscles in the world, and that allowed him to finally be happy again.

Borderline Personality Disorder (BPD)

❖

Eve's Story

Sometimes life presents you with challenges that make no sense. What you do with such challenges will determine who and what you become in life.

Eve was an energetic young girl who was always full of life and energy. She loved spending time outside and playing games at every opportunity. She liked going for walks in the woods with her dog and always tried to meet up with her friends whenever she could. Unfortunately, Eve's state of positivity wouldn't last forever.

One day, Eve was out in her garden, running around with her pet dog, Misty. "Wait for me!" Eve shouted joyfully, as she tried to catch up with Misty. Suddenly a grey cloud swept over Eve's garden, replacing the clear blue skies that had been there just moments before.

The change in the weather flicked a switch in Eve's brain. Suddenly she didn't feel happy anymore.

"Eve! Come in! It's starting to rain!" Eve's mother called from inside the house, anxious for her daughter not to get wet. Eve didn't respond. She just stood there, rooted to the spot, unable to summon the energy to go back to the house. She didn't care that it was raining and she was getting wet. She didn't care about anything.

Suddenly, Eve felt a rush of happiness and started to sing and dance in the rain! "Come outside and dance with me, Mom! It's like having a shower!" she cried.

"Eve, you come in right now before you catch a cold! I won't tell you again!" Eve's mother shouted, who was getting a little annoyed at her daughter for fooling around in the rain.

"You're no fun!" Eve laughed, as she called Misty and ran inside.

"Eve, what were you thinking? Jumping around like that in the rain! Do you want to get sick? Don't do that again. Do you hear me?" Eve's mother said, with a stern look on her face.

For the second time that day, a switch flicked in Eve's head, and suddenly anger replaced happiness. 'Shut up!' she roared, 'You never let me do anything!'

and she ran upstairs to her room, slamming her bedroom door as she went inside. Eve screamed at the top of her lungs. She felt so angry! She looked at her perfectly tidy room and got even angrier. She took all her neatly folded clothes out of her wardrobe and threw them on the floor! Then she knocked all the ornaments off her shelf and ripped a poster off the wall, tearing it in half. Eve stood in the middle of her room panting, looking at the mess she had just made. Messing up her room had made her feel a little bit better, it made her a little less angry.

Eve's mood swings continued for the next couple of weeks and her moods would change without warning. Her parents started to feel as if they were walking on eggshells around their daughter and couldn't understand how she could be happy one minute, and then suddenly be sad or angry the next. Eve didn't know why her moods changed so much either. And she couldn't tell what was causing it.

Eve's mood swings weren't the only thing that was different about her. One day, Eve would push her parents away, not wanting to talk to anyone, and the next she would beg them not to leave her side. One day, she would tell them how much she hated them, and the next she would tell them that she loved them more than anything in the whole world.

"Eve, I'm going to go into town shopping. I'll see you later, okay?" Eve's mother said one morning.

"Okay, bye!" Eve yelled back from her bedroom.

Fifteen minutes after Eve's mother had left the house to go shopping, Eve started thinking to herself, 'What if she doesn't come back? What if she never wants to see me again?' With that, she began to panic. She picked up her phone and texted 'Where are you?' to her mother and checked every thirty seconds to see if she had received a text back.

Less than an hour later, Eve heard the front door of her house open and feet rush up the stairs. She looked over towards her bedroom door as her mother came running in.

"Are you okay? What's wrong?!" Eve's mother asked, worried that something had happened to Eve while she was away.

"Nothing's wrong. I'm okay. But I thought you had left me forever..." Eve said, not making eye contact with her.

"Eve, I was only gone for just over an hour! In that time, I received five text messages and ten missed calls. I left my phone in the car and was worried sick when I finally saw it. I told you I had a little bit of shopping to do."

"I know, I just missed you. And I love you. I don't want you to leave me..."

"You don't ever have to worry about me leaving you. I'll always be here," Eve's mother said, as she went over to her daughter to give her a hug. "I love you too."

The next day after Eve had lunch with her parents, her father asked her to clean up after them.

"No. You do it!" Eve snapped. She wasn't in the mood for a conversation or to do any housework.

"Eve. You had lunch made for you. I think it's only fair that you clean up," her dad said.

"Leave me alone! I didn't even want lunch. You're always telling me to do things! I hate it! I hate both of you! I never want to see you again. I'm leaving!" Eve shouted as she ran out the door and down the road with her dog, Misty, running behind her.

Eve ran to her local park and sat down on a bench. Misty sensed that she was upset and put her head on Eve's legs. "It's just me and you, Misty," Eve said, as she stroked Misty's soft fur. "Everyone else hates us and we hate them." Eve sat on the park bench for two hours as she just thought about how much she never wanted to see her parents ever again. Eventually her anger disappeared, and she returned home and apologized to her parents for storming out of the house before eating the dinner that was on the kitchen table waiting for her.

Concerned over their daughter's behaviour, Eve's parents decided to go out for a family walk in the woods, where they were hoping they could talk to Eve to find out if anything was troubling her. During the walk Eve rarely walked alongside her parents, choosing instead to run ahead with Misty. Beside the trail that the family were walking along was a river, which was slowly flowing in the same direction they were walking in.

"Mom! Dad! Look at me! I'm going swimming!" Eve shouted from up the road.

"Eve, don't you dare –" Eve's mother started calling, but before she could finish the sentence, Eve had jumped into the waist-deep river.

"Eve!" her mother screamed, rushing over.

Eve started to laugh as she splashed around in the water. Misty was also in the water, swimming in circles around Eve. Eve didn't have a spare change of clothes and it was a long walk back to the car. It wasn't a warm day and the water was freezing cold. She hadn't thought it through before jumping into the river. One minute, she was running along the track and the next, she way diving into a freezing cold river! Eve climbed out and looked at her parents. "Can we please go home? I'm freezing!" she moaned, as she turned back to the car.

Over the next few days, Eve's behaviour became more and more out of control. One day, she decided to jump out of her bedroom window onto the grass outside. She was lucky she didn't break her leg! Another day, when she was out shopping with her mother, she decided to start sliding up and down the floor. "Mom slide with me! It's so much fun!" she screamed, not caring that other people in the shop were staring at her. Sensing that all was not well, Eve's parents decided that they would take her to a doctor to talk about her unusual behaviour and get advice on what to do.

The next day, Eve went to the doctor with her parents. Together, they explained to the doctor how Eve had been acting for the past couple of months. They told him about how her moods would change from happy to sad to angry as though at the flick of a switch. They told him how Eve would tell them that she loved and needed them one day and push them away the next. They informed him how Eve would do things without thinking, like jumping into an ice-cold river on a mild day.

The doctor took a moment to reflect, after hearing everything Eve's family had to say, before finally turning to Eve, to say, "Eve, everything is going to be okay. What you have just described sounds like Borderline Personality Disorder, or BPD. People with BPD see the world in black and white, and often miss out on all the grey in between. Your mood changes are not your fault, even if they don't make any sense to you."

He continued, "People with BPD often have a harder time maintaining stable moods and even relationships with other people. One day, you might say you hate someone and the next you'll say that you love them and that you need them. Imagine, if you will, someone walking on a tightrope trying to find balance. And now imagine another person on that tightrope, but that person has a wall beside them to help them balance whenever they need it. People with BPD are like the person walking on the tightrope without a wall to help them balance, so life may seem a little more out of their control from time to time.

I am going to give you an appointment to see me in three days' time. And I will see you twice a week every week for the next couple of months. And we'll talk more about your BPD and we'll come up with ways to manage it. Does that sound okay?"

"It does," said Eve, unsure how she felt about seeing a doctor twice a week when she didn't feel like there was anything wrong with her. But she would do it.

That night, Eve found herself alone in her bedroom. She was thinking about everything the doctor had said. Suddenly she got up and stood at the centre of her room. She closed her eyes and tried to balance. After only a couple of seconds she lost her balance and had to open her eyes to stop herself from falling! Next, she did the same exercise but beside the wall. Every time she felt like she was about to lose balance, she was able to put her hand on the wall to keep her steady. This was the point the doctor was making when she was with him in his office. Eve was glad that she could use the doctor as a wall to help her find balance in her life.

Over the next couple of months, Eve saw her doctor and started to learn more about BPD and how to find balance. During one of her sessions, her doctor said something that stuck in Eve's brain. "There is no shame in reaching out for someone to catch you if you feel as though you're about to fall." Eve knew she had a lot more to learn about BPD, but she also knew that whatever she was going to go through in life, she didn't have to go through it alone.

Bullying

Andy's Story

To pick on someone smaller than you is not an act of strength, but an act of weakness.

Andy was a strong, talented boy who lived each day as if it were his last. He got good grades in school and was the best player on the school football and hurling teams. He was always surrounded by friends wherever he went. Everyone in school liked Andy, or so he thought.

One day, when Andy was walking into the classroom at the start of school, he saw a group of boys looking at him and whispering. Just as Andy was about to approach them to say hello, the bell rang and the boys left to go to their tables, glancing at each other with mischievous grins on their faces as they left. 'That was odd,' Andy thought to himself. He could have sworn that it looked like they were talking about him when they were huddled together in their group.

At lunchtime, when everyone in the class was playing football in the schoolyard, Andy rushed over to join them. He loved football and was the best in the class.

"Go away! This is my ball and you can't play!" said Tyler, one of the boys from Andy's class.

"Please let me play," Andy begged. He had been looking forward to playing football at lunch time all day.

"No, we have enough players already. Go away."

With his head bowed and his hands in his pockets, Andy walked away, confused as to why Tyler wasn't allowing him to play.

The next day at school, no one from Andy's class spoke to him. Tyler and the other boys called him names, like 'stupid' and 'loser' and everyone was afraid to stick up for Andy in case Tyler would start calling them names too. Tyler was the biggest and strongest boy in the class, and no one dared to get on his bad side. But Andy hadn't done anything to Tyler. Tyler was being mean to him for no reason.

As the days passed by, Andy began to feel more and more alone. Tyler, the class bully, was making his life a living hell and had started to turn some of the other members of the class against him too. Apart from calling Andy names, Tyler had begun to bully Andy in other ways, too. Whenever Andy was sitting at his table and the teacher was out of the room, Tyler would approach Andy's table and knock over his books. At lunchtime, Tyler would take the sandwiches that Andy's mother made him every day for lunch and eat them himself. Andy would go the entire day without eating. Sometimes Andy's stomach would growl towards the end of the school day because he was so hungry and everyone in the classroom would laugh at him, leaving Andy feeling embarrassed and humiliated.

One day after school, Andy was on his own outside the school waiting for his mother to pick him up. She was late. Suddenly, Tyler and his friends came out of school. They had had to stay back in class after the final bell because they had gotten in trouble.

"What are you still doing here? Your mom doesn't want to collect a loser like you?" Tyler sneered, with his friends snickering behind him.

"Leave me alone! I'm tired of you picking on me," Andy said, trying not to sound intimidated.

"Or what? Are you going to do something? You'll do nothing," Tyler said, and he pushed Andy to the ground. "I'm bigger and stronger than you are. And don't you forget that, you little wimp."

Andy picked himself up off the ground and dusted himself off as Tyler and his friends walked away together, laughing.

Later that evening, Andy's mother noticed the cuts on his arms and asked how he got them. Afraid of what Tyler might do to him if he told, Andy lied to her and said that he had tripped over a rock and fallen.

"Okay," his mother sighed. "Just try to be more careful next time."

That night, Andy was in his room doing his Maths homework when he received a text message. He looked down at his phone. It was a message from Tyler. "No one at school likes you, loser!" it read. Andy threw his phone on the floor and tried to concentrate on his homework. But he couldn't get the thoughts of what was going on in school out of his head.

The next morning, Andy's mother opened his bedroom door to call him to get up for school. "I can't go to school today. I have a pain in my stomach. I'm sick," Andy moaned, coughing to make his lie seem more believable.

"Okay," his mother said, "I'll ring the school and let them know that you won't be in today. Try and get some rest so you'll be well enough to go in tomorrow."

That night, Andy received another message from Tyler. "School was much better without you today. You should stay at home more often." it read. Andy turned his phone off and lay face down on his bed and started to cry. Why was this happening to him? What had he done to deserve this?

Andy decided to stay home from school the next day too. When he finally came out of his room in the afternoon, he was in no mood to talk to anyone.

"Andy, would you like me to make you something to eat?" his mother asked him, with a concerned look on her face.

"No! I don't want anything, leave me alone!" Andy snapped.

Andy's mother decided to let his poor attitude slide, he had a stomach bug after all, or so she thought.

Over the coming weeks, Andy continued to take his bad moods out on his parents and his little brother and sister. At school, he didn't have anyone to talk to because no one wanted to be the next person bullied by Tyler and his friends. Tyler had sent out a warning to everyone in the class that if anyone helped Andy, he would bully them, too. As a result, Andy found himself spending more and more time alone.

Andy spent lunchtimes alone in the school bathrooms to avoid Tyler and all of Tyler's friends. During class Andy was too afraid to put his hand up to answer the teacher's questions. He kept his head down and tried to go unnoticed as much as he possibly could. At the end of school Andy would leave the building as quickly as he could so he wouldn't see Tyler on his way out.

Andy wished he could go to a different school. He wished he could run away and never come back. Sometimes he felt terribly alone, other times he was angry and blamed himself for everything that was going on. When Andy felt like this, he hurt himself, by punching the wall over and over again, sometimes even making his knuckles bleed. He had had enough. All he wanted was for Tyler to stop bullying him. He wanted everything to go back to the way it used to be. But he didn't know how to make that happen.

On one hot Saturday afternoon, Andy was playing football outside of his house, using the walls of the house as a target. He kicked the ball as hard as he could against the wall, narrowly missing the window. Andy's dad came outside, annoyed with Andy for kicking the football too close to the windows.

"Be careful!" Andy's dad warned. "Stop kicking

that ball so hard towards the house. You could break a window! And who will be left paying for that?"

"I'm not kicking it hard. Leave me alone!" Andy snapped, as he smacked the ball towards the house again.

"That's it. I've had enough of your bad attitude lately. You have been rude to everyone in the house for weeks. Tell me what's causing your bad behaviour."

"I don't want to talk about it, okay?!" Andy shouted, as he stormed back inside the house.

"Don't walk away from me while I'm talking to you," his dad said, following him inside.

"Leave me alone! Why can't anyone just leave me alone?" Andy roared, but when he turned around to face his father, he wasn't angry – he was sad, and had tears of sadness in his eyes. "I have a problem," he said, "and I don't know what to do about it." And with that, he started to cry.

"Sit down. I'll make us both a cup of tea and we can talk about this problem of yours," Andy's dad said, as he turned the kettle on and took out two cups from the press.

For the next hour, Andy and his dad talked about everything that had been going on at school recently. They talked about how Tyler would call him names and even hit him. How he would take his lunch, leaving Andy starving with nothing to eat all day at school. How he would knock over the books on his desk. They talked about how no one would help Andy because they were afraid of what Tyler might to do them if they did. They spoke about the text messages Andy received every day and how he was beginning to feel like he was a worthless loser, just like Tyler said he was.

When Andy's dad told him what to do, Andy couldn't believe his ears. Andy wanted revenge! But instead Andy's dad told him that he needed to be the bigger person, and to sort out his issues with Tyler without violence. "To attack someone smaller than you is not an act of strength, but an act of weakness. True strength is seeing others in need and finding the courage to help them. While you may think Tyler may be the biggest and strongest in your class, deep down, he's not. He is the weakest. One day he will learn this for himself. And it may be too late for him when he does."

The next day, Andy's dad went to the school and set up an appointment with Andy's teacher and Tyler's father. Andy and Tyler also attended. During the meeting, Andy saw his bully break down in tears and apologize to him. He said that one of the boys in the year above was bullying him and that made him feel small, weak, and afraid. He said that he didn't want everyone in the class to think he was weak so he decided to pick on Andy, even though he actually liked Andy. He admitted that he was wrong, and that he would do whatever he could to make it up to Andy. After hearing everything Tyler had to say, Andy chose to take his father's advice about being the bigger person and forgave Tyler.

Over time, Andy and Tyler overcame their issues and became close friends. Andy was finally happy and able to enjoy life at school again. He realized that Tyler was not a bad person, he was just someone who was struggling himself, and had responded in the wrong way. Whenever Andy and Tyler saw another kid in school getting bullied, they would step in and tell the bully that picking on someone smaller and weaker is not brave or strong, but the opposite. Andy and Tyler even talked to the teachers and helped set up an anti-bullying group that talked to the whole school, explaining why bullying is wrong.

Andy experienced something no one should ever have to experience, but he had learned a valuable lesson that would stay with him everywhere he went in life. Strength does not come from being the biggest and the strongest. True strength comes from being able to accept your weaknesses and keep moving forward. It's about being able to pick yourself up again, even when you get knocked down over and over. And that, for Andy, would make all the difference in living a happy life.

Bulimia

Hope's Story

Never try to be someone that you're not. Be you and be the best you that you can be.

Hope was an intelligent young girl who loved to write poetry and song lyrics and watch movies. She loved to dance and went to ballet lessons every weekend. She was shy but friendly to everyone. "One day I'm going to be a somebody," she would say.

One day at school, one of Hope's classmates named Sarah had her lunch taken by one of the boys as a joke. When Sarah asked who took her lunch, the boys told her that they saw Hope take it. Sarah approached Hope and asked for her lunch back. When Hope said that she didn't take her lunch, Sarah didn't believe her and got angry.

"Liar!" Sarah screamed. "Everyone said that they saw you take my lunch!"

"I swear! I didn't take it! You're making a mistake!" Hope said, who had just been sitting at her desk minding her own business.

"You're lying, and you know it! You took it, and I bet you ate it too, you fatty!" Sarah shouted in front of the whole class, as she walked away.

Hope was shocked and couldn't hold in her tears. Why would Sarah call her fat? Hope had never considered herself fat before. Was she? Did everyone else in the class think she was fat, too?

When Hope came home that day after school, she went straight to the bathroom, took off her school jumper and looked at her reflection in the mirror. She stared into the mirror for what seemed like an eternity. She looked at her body from the front and side. She grabbed the fat on her stomach in disgust. In that moment, Hope felt fat and dirty. She wanted to lose weight so the other girls in her class wouldn't think she was fat anymore.

Over the next few days, Hope grew more and more concerned with the way she looked. She would look at the other girls in her class and often compare how she looked to the way they looked. She never told any of her friends she was worried that she was fat because she was afraid they might agree with her.

Sarah eventually found out that the boys had taken her lunch as a joke and apologized to Hope for blaming her. "I'm sorry for blaming you and calling you fat. I don't know why I said it because you're not fat at all!" she said. Hope forgave Sarah and they became friends again. However, Hope still hated the way she looked and still thought she was fat and needed to lose weight.

One day, Hope had a stomach bug and couldn't go to school. She was so sick that she couldn't eat any food and had to rush to the bathroom on occasion to throw up. After three days of being sick, she finally felt better. When she saw her reflection in the mirror, she couldn't believe her eyes! She had lost so much weight while she was sick. She was very happy with how she looked and wished she could stay that way forever.

As she started to feel better again, Hope's appetite came back, and she soon returned to her normal weight. Hope was miserable that she had put the weight back on, and she wished she could lose it all again. She remembered how she hadn't eaten while she was sick and how she had thrown up a few times a day. "What if I stopped eating and made myself throw up? Maybe I could be skinny then?" Hope said to herself.

That night after Hope had eaten her dinner, she went to the bathroom. She looked at her reflection in the mirror and took a deep breath. She was nervous and a little ashamed of herself for what she was about to do. She walked towards the toilet and started to play music on her phone to drown out any noise she was about to make. She kneeled in front of the toilet bowl and stuck two of her fingers down her throat. As her fingers went further down her throat, the food she had just eaten came back out. When Hope was finished, she didn't feel ashamed like she thought she would – instead, she felt relieved! She flushed the toilet and rinsed her mouth out in the sink before leaving the bathroom again.

Hope decided that she wouldn't eat for the next couple of days so she could lose more weight. She didn't eat again that night, skipped breakfast in the morning, and threw her school lunch into the bin the following day. However, the next night, Hope was so hungry that she gave in to the temptation to eat. She decided to eat some of her dinner. "Just one or two bites can't hurt, can they?" she said.

Hope took a bite of her food. It was delicious. She took another bite, and another, and another. Before she knew it, she had eaten all of her dinner! But Hope wasn't finished eating. She opened the press and grabbed all the biscuits she could find. Before she had even realized it, she had eaten all of them! She felt ashamed of herself for eating so much food and went to the bathroom to make herself throw up, to make up for what she had just done. She felt a little less ashamed of herself after she did that.

Over the next few weeks, Hope would stuff her face with lots and lots of food and then run to the bathroom to make herself get sick. She would do this up to five times a day! She hid her behaviour as much as possible from the rest of the world. It was her little secret that no one could ever know about. At home, she would eat alone and play music while she was throwing up in the bathroom, or she would find somewhere outside the house to do it. Hope took money from her mom's purse when her mom wasn't looking, to buy sweets and cake and anything else she wanted to buy at the shop to eat in one go. Then she threw it all up again shortly after.

Hope also began to exercise every day. Every morning she would get up while her parents were still asleep and would run for an hour. If one day she didn't get sick, she ran for two hours the next day to make up for it.

Hope hated herself for what she was doing, but she couldn't stop. She needed to be skinny! She was jealous of the other girls in her class who were skinny and every day at school she would look at them all, wishing that one day she could look like them. Every time Hope passed a mirror, she would stop and look at what she thought was a fat, disgusting girl staring back at her. When Hope was at home, she spent hours on the computer looking at thin, beautiful women. "Why can't I look like that?" she moaned.

Hope was so ashamed of herself for what she was doing that she began to punish herself. She thought she was weak and pathetic and didn't deserve nice things. She stopped wearing her nice clothes and wore old, baggy clothes instead. When her friends asked her to go outside with them, she refused because she felt she didn't deserve to have fun with friends. She wouldn't even allow herself to sleep in her bed and slept on her floor instead. "When I'm skinny and beautiful, I'll let myself have nice things," she promised herself.

Over time, Hope's parents started to notice that their daughter would go places on her own without telling anyone where she was going. They were worried that something was wrong with her, but she wouldn't tell them what it was.

One day, when Hope went outside to throw up after eating a lot of food, she didn't realize that her mother was also outside, watching her from the end of the garden. As Hope was about to make herself throw up, her mother screamed, "Hope! What on earth do you think you're doing?!"

Hope froze on the spot. She didn't know what to say. She had been caught just as she was about to make herself throw up, so she couldn't lie. Her secret was finally about to be exposed. She had two choices: she could tell the truth, or she could try to come up with another lie. Bravely, she decided to tell the truth.

Hope told her mother everything, from overeating to making herself throw up. She told her about how she would go for a run before anyone was awake every morning and how she would look at good-looking, skinny women on the internet for hours at a time, wishing that she were them. She even told her how she slept on the floor because she didn't think she deserved a bed. She said she did all of these things because she thought that she was fat.

"I just want to be skinny and beautiful!" Hope cried.

"But you are both of those things and more!" Hope's mother replied.

"I'm not! I'm fat and disgusting and I bet everyone else thinks so, too," Hope said, crying even more.

"Hope, honey, no one is perfect," her mother said, "but everyone's special and unique in their own way. Don't ever compare the way you look to the way someone else does because there is only one of them, just like there is only one of you. I've always said that you're just like me when I was your age and you are. I used to think that I was fat and I hated how I looked, too. And, to tell you the truth, some days I look in the mirror and still see a fat, ugly woman staring back at me."

"But you're so skinny!" Hope gasped.

"I know, but some days my mind likes to play games with me and tells me that I'm fat, no matter how thin I really am."

"So how can I learn not to be sad about myself, like you aren't?" Hope asked. She was shocked to learn that sometimes her mom hated the way she looked and thought she was fat, just like she did. Hope always believed she was the only one who had these bad thoughts.

"You just have to accept that you will never look exactly the same as anyone else. But that's what's so special about you, there is only one of you and there only ever will be one of you. Everyone has insecurities, but no one likes to talk about them. Right now, there could be a girl who hates herself and is crying herself to sleep every night because all she wants in the world is to look just like you," Hope's mother said.

"I just want to be a somebody. One day I promise that I will be..." Hope mumbled.

Stopping her daughter mid-sentence and taking her by the hand, Hope's mother said, "You already are. And when you see the strong, amazing young girl you already are right now, then I promise you that you'll be able to move past these difficult moments."

Over the next few months, Hope learned to accept who she was and how she looked. She stopped comparing herself to other girls and looking in the mirror every time she passed one. She stopped punishing herself and slept in her own bed again, wore her nice clothes again and went out with her friends again. She stopped eating large amounts of food in one sitting and stopped forcing herself to throw up to lose weight. It wasn't easy, and some days she nearly gave up. But she didn't. She was strong and brave and learned to fight her inner monsters one day at a time.

Hope finally understood that everyone was different in their own, unique way. There was only one of Hope and there would only ever be one of her, and that made her feel special. Every time she looked in the mirror, she didn't see a fat, disgusting girl in her reflection, but a thin, beautiful girl smiling back at her instead. Hope realized that she had always been a somebody, even if she didn't know it at the time, and that made her happy. And she was ready to show the rest of the world who she really was.

Psychosis

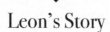

Leon's Story

Open your eyes and then you will find
The secret world that exists in your mind.

Leon was a determined young boy who dreamed of one day being famous. He was a gymnast and was extremely competitive. He could do backflips, cartwheels and somersaults. He could hold a handstand for a full minute. He dreamed of one day representing Ireland in gymnastics at the Olympics.

One day at gymnastics practice, Leon's coach told the team about an upcoming competition in July, just over three months away. Leon had already competed in this competition twice before and had come second both times. But now he was better than ever. This time he really believed that he would win. He had trained the hardest he had ever trained after coming second in the competition for the second time, and he was willing to train even harder again. 'Nothing will stop me from winning the trophy this time,' he thought.

With the competition drawing closer, Leon trained early every morning and late every night. He was so excited that he couldn't sleep, even though the competition was still months away! "I can't wait to show everyone how much I've improved this year. This time, I'm going to win!" Leon said to himself. He trained and trained, and with each passing day, he slept less and less.

As the weeks passed, Leon was training all day and only getting two or three hours of sleep a night. One night, he didn't sleep at all. Because he wasn't getting any sleep, he was having trouble at home, at school and even at training. At home, he was snapping at his family. At school, he couldn't concentrate and was having trouble staying awake in class. And at training, he wasn't able to perform at his best. But this only made him push himself harder than ever.

During the holidays Leon was able to train even more. The competition was only a month away and Leon needed to make every second of every day count.

One fine summer's day, Leon was outside in his garden doing backflips under the heat of the sun. He hadn't slept in two days. He was exhausted, but he couldn't afford to sleep. He had to win the competition! He had to train as much as he possibly could. There was no way he was going to come second three years in a row.

As he was training, Leon heard a noise in the bushes. When he looked over his shoulder, he saw a bird fly off one of the trees in the back garden. Leon suddenly felt as if he wasn't alone. He grabbed a stick and went over to the bushes he had heard the noise come from. There was nothing there. Still, Leon suspected that he was being watched while he was exercising, and he had a feeling that he knew who it was. 'The other gymnastics team are afraid because they know how much better I've gotten,' he thought. 'And now they're sending people to spy on me while I train. What cheaters!'

When Leon was at gymnastics training that night, he was so tired from training all day and not sleeping that he kept making mistakes.

"Leon! Get your act together!" his coach yelled.

"Sorry coach!" Leon said. "I'm just having an off day."

"The competition is next month. You can't afford to have any off days!"

"Come on Leon. You've got this," Leon said to himself on the gymnastics mat. "One, two, three..." He took off running and did two cartwheels followed by a backflip! He was very happy with that.

"Much better!" his coach yelled, applauding him. He had been watching his star pupil in action.

That night while Leon was walking home, he kept looking over his shoulder. 'Is someone following me?' he thought to himself. How scared did Leon's rivals have to be to send people to spy on him?

Leon decided to write down all the places and times he had been followed or felt like he was being watched by his rival's gymnastics team. Less than a month before the competition, Leon wrote the following into his journal:

> This is going to sound crazy, and I am not crazy, but I still haven't found the answer to why whenever I bring my dog outside for a walk or go outside to do gymnastics in my garden, I feel like I am being watched. I think the rival gymnastics team is secretly watching me. They're scared. They know that I'm going to win this year and they are doing everything they can to learn my secrets so they can beat me. I am not crazy. I am not making this up. But I'm afraid that if I tell anyone what is happening that they will laugh at me and won't believe me.

"Leon, me and your dad are bringing the dog out for a walk. We'll be back in an hour. See you then," Leon's mother said, as they left Leon in an empty house for the next hour.

Happy that he had a whole hour to himself, Leon decided to take full advantage of the free house and look for any signs that the rival gymnastics team had been in his house spying on him. He walked around his entire house, checking every room. He looked in every press and wardrobe, taking out clothes, pots, pans, cups, and plates in the process, to see if there were any cameras hidden anywhere to spy on him while he trained. 'Nothing there. They're good. They've left no evidence that they were here,' Leon thought to himself.

"Leon, why is the house in such a mess? Clean it up right now!" Leon's mother screamed at him when she and Leon's dad came back from their walk with the dog.

"I will. Sorry," Leon said, not really listening to her. He was too busy thinking of what other ways his rivals could be spying on him.

As time went on, Leon became less and less concerned about the gymnastics competition, and more concerned about the people who were spying on him.

Leon was exhausted and was sleeping less than ever before. He had lost his appetite. Some days he would go the entire day without eating. He wrote in his diary every day about whether he felt like he was being watched or followed on that particular day. Every time someone looked at him, he worried that they were a spy from his rival's gymnastics team. Any time he heard a noise around him, he would think that there was someone hiding somewhere, watching him. Leon was so distracted during gymnastics practice that one day his coach told him to go home to get some rest instead.

When the day of the competition arrived, Leon was completely worn-out. All he had been able to think about in the weeks leading up to it had been that people were watching him, and he had barely trained because of it.

"Hey Leon. Good luck today!" one of the boys from a rival gymnastics team said.

'Yeah right. Is that why you were spying on me with the rest of your team? Trying to cheat and find out my secrets?' Leon thought.

At the end of the competition Leon came in eighteenth place out of twenty. He was devastated! The best place Leon's rivals could manage was third place. In fact, two of Leon's teammates came first and second.

"What happened with you today?" Leon's teammate, who had come first asked. "You've been the best gymnast in our club all year, you should have won! You didn't even make the top ten."

Leon didn't answer. He knew his teammate was right. Leon knew that he was better than him. He knew that he was the best gymnast at the tournament. He knew that he had missed out on his chance to come first and win the trophy. He was angry at himself for not winning and angry at the rival gymnastics team for spying on him. Leon believed that if people hadn't been watching him wherever he went, he would have won.

The next day, Leon heard a knock on the door. It was his coach and the family doctor. He wondered if something was wrong. Leon's coach, his parents and the doctor sat down with Leon. His parents had rung his coach and doctor and asked them to come over because they were very concerned about their son. Leon's coach said that he was very worried about him too, and that he had noticed that Leon hadn't been himself for months.

Leon decided to come clean. What was the worst that could happen? He hadn't been to bed since the competition and he was sick of looking over his shoulder all the time to see if someone was following him.

Leon told his parents, coach and doctor everything. He told them that his rivals were following him; that they would hide behind the bushes in the garden while he was training and that they were somehow spying on him in his house. When he had finished, he was shocked at what everyone said next.

"No one's been spying on you," Leon's mother said.

"You haven't been yourself at all lately. I think your mind is playing tricks on you," his dad said.

Leon looked at everyone. His coach agreed with his parents. The doctor agreed with his parents. Why didn't anyone believe him?

"Leon, how many hours of sleep have you been getting recently?" the doctor asked.

"One, maybe two hours a night for the last couple of weeks. But what difference does that make? There are people spying on me!"

"Have you been eating? Training?" the doctor asked.

"I haven't had time to eat. And of course, I train all day. I need to be the best. Right, coach?" His coach didn't reply. "Why aren't any of you listening to me?! There have been people spying on me!" Leon couldn't believe that everyone seemed more interested in how much sleep he was getting instead of the people who had been spying on him for months!

The doctor then explained to Leon that because his brain was so tired from not sleeping, from training so much and because he wasn't feeding his body with much food, his brain had started to give him ideas that Leon would normally know straight away weren't true. But because Leon was so tired, these thoughts and ideas that came to him, no matter how ridiculous they sounded when said out loud, seemed much more realistic than they really were. The doctor said that no one was following or spying on Leon, but that he understood if Leon didn't believe him right away. "It isn't easy when you find out that your mind is telling you lies," he said. But he said that throughout the next year, he would be working with Leon to help him see that what he had thought his rivals were doing to him right now wasn't really happening.

Six months later, Leon was a very different boy to the one he had been. He was still doing gymnastics, but he was getting much more sleep and eating more throughout the day. On top of this, Leon was also seeing his doctor to help him whenever he felt that his mind was playing tricks on him. Leon now knew that because he hadn't been taking care of his body or mind before the competition, his mind had given him ideas that he thought were true, but actually weren't. No one had ever been spying on Leon, he realized that now.

Leon was happy that his mind was back on his side again, and he had learned a valuable lesson. As he walked to gymnastics training one evening he smiled to himself, because he knew one thing for sure – he would never, ever not take care of his brain the right way, ever again.

Post-Traumatic Stress Disorder (PTSD)

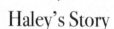

Haley's Story

Hope has found her at last,
She'll leave the past in the past.

Haley was a polite, hard-working young girl who kept to herself. Although she was very mannerly whenever she would talk to someone, she was very quiet and shy. She found solace in doing things on her own. She loved reading science books and finding out interesting new facts about the world. She played the piano and the violin and went to Irish dancing practice at the weekends. She always gave her all to everything she did. But Haley had experienced a great tragedy in her life, and she lived with the pain from it every day.

When Haley was just four years old, her mother died in a car accident. Haley and her father were severely injured in the same accident. While they were driving home late one cold, wet, foggy night, their car hit a bump on the road and slid around in circles for what seemed like an eternity. The next thing that Haley saw were the headlights of a truck coming towards the car. It approached the car in slow motion and Haley heard her mother cry "Nooo!" as she threw herself across Haley, protecting her daughter and saving her life. The next thing Haley remembered was waking up in a hospital, surrounded by crying family members. Her father stood over her, smiling, with tears in his eyes, and just said, "Welcome back, Angel. I love you so much."

Six years later, a ten-year-old Haley and her father lived in a small cottage in the country. Every day, the memory of what happened on that cold, wet, foggy night haunted Haley. Every time she saw a truck she would freeze, and stand rooted to the spot. It would take her a couple of moments to calm down. When her dad wanted to go somewhere with her in the car, she would look for excuses not to go. She would say that it was too wet or too dark to drive. "It's too dangerous to drive today Dad, stay here and be safe. Drive your car tomorrow," she would beg her dad. If her dad was driving home and was running late, she would panic and ring him to make sure he was okay.

One night, Haley had a dream that she was up in the sky, floating above the clouds. She looked down at all the houses below her. They looked so small! The birds flew past her and Haley laughed with glee as she tried to keep up with them. She was having the time of her life and she never wanted to stop flying. Suddenly, the clouds turned grey and the sound of thunder filled the sky. It started to rain and Haley started falling. "Aaahhh!" she screamed.

Bang! Haley landed on a seat. She looked around. She was in the back seat of a car. But this car looked familiar. Suddenly, a blonde woman in the front seat turned around to her and smiled. "Hi Angel," she said, "I see you're awake from your nap!" Haley recognised this blonde woman – it was her mother! Suddenly, the car hit something on the road and lost control. The car spun around and around, and a loud beeping noise filled the air. "Haley!" Haley's mother screamed, throwing herself in front of her daughter. Haley froze and gasped in horror as she watched the bright lights of a truck rapidly approaching...

"Nooo!" Haley woke up screaming.

"Haley, what is it?" her dad cried, rushing into her room.

"Dad, I had a dream. I was flying and then I fell. And then I saw Mom, and then..." Haley couldn't finish her sentence, as her dad grabbed her to give her a hug.

"It's okay. I've got you. You're okay. I'm right here," he said, reassuring his daughter as she began to calm down.

"Dad, promise me you'll never leave me," Haley said.

"I promise. I'll always be here for you. I love you," her dad said, as he kissed the top of her head.

Before she knew it, Haley was having the same nightmare every night, reliving her mother's death on that cold, wet, foggy night. Haley would wake up night after night in tears, with her body shaking and her heart racing. She was terrified of her nightmare and would always try to stay awake in bed for as long as she could every night, so she wouldn't have to face it again.

Haley became much more nervous and timid after experiencing her nightmare for the first time. She had always been a shy girl who found comfort in her own company, but now she needed to be alone because she felt afraid all the time. At school, she could no longer concentrate in class, and her teacher would always catch her staring out the window, out the door or anywhere else in the classroom other than at the blackboard. At home, Haley jumped at any sudden noises. If she heard a strange noise in another room, she would worry that there was someone or something in the house that shouldn't be there.

One day, Haley was walking home with her dad. As they were crossing the road, Haley froze on the spot and screamed, "Dad, no!"

"What is it?" her dad asked, getting a fright.

"The truck!" Haley cried, with tears in her eyes and her legs shaking.

"There's nothing's there. No car or truck has passed us in the last five minutes. Are you feeling okay?"

"But I saw it! Right there!" Haley said, pointing her shaking finger at a spot on the road. "I saw the lights. I heard the noise of the cars. Right there!" Haley couldn't hold her tears in any longer and they started flowing down her face. She was so sure that a truck had just sped past her and her dad as they were about to cross the road. She had just saved both of their lives, hadn't she?

Over the next couple of months, Haley became more and more easily startled. She had nightmares every night, where she would wake up in a panic. Sometimes during the day, she would see a truck's headlights coming her way before vanishing into thin air. She would jump at any sudden noises and was constantly looking over her shoulder to make sure that she was safe. In her mind, danger was always lurking just around the corner waiting to catch her off guard. Haley was completely exhausted and just wanted it all to stop. Her father noticed that she was miserable, but nothing he said or did seemed to help.

One summer's night, Haley's dad called her outside to the garden. Haley wasn't sure what it was but there was something magical about the night. There was a full moon above her and the sky was covered with twinkling stars. There was a warmth in the air which was rare to feel at night.

"There's a big world out there. It really makes you think," her dad said.

"Think about what?" Haley asked.

"The future. You can be anything you want to be, you know," her dad replied.

"I miss Mom. I keep seeing her at night. I wish I could see her again. I wish she never jumped in front of me to save me. If she hadn't, then maybe she would still be alive. It's all my fault..." Haley said, as she broke down in tears. She was so sad and tired of feeling this way and she couldn't hold it in any longer.

"Haley, listen to me. Your mother loved you more than anything in this world. It is not your fault. Never think like that," Haley's father said, putting his arms around his daughter to comfort her.

This was the first time Haley had ever brought up her mother's death and the accident by herself. She always avoided talking about it. It was as if she was afraid to admit the accident had even happened. Haley and her dad spent the next hour under the stars talking about everything Haley had been going through lately. Haley told her father about her nightmares. She told him about seeing the headlights of the truck at different times of the day. She told him about being frightened every time she was in a car. She told him everything that she was sad and worried about. Haley cried, and her dad was there to comfort her.

"Your mother is still alive, you know. She lives right here." Haley's dad said, pointing to his daughter's heart. "You have her eyes and her smile, and you even share her love of science. When I look at you, I see your mother. She lives in you."

With those words, Haley looked up to the stars, as if she was expecting to see her mother smiling down at her. She felt a warmth in her heart that she hadn't felt in a long, long time. Fear and loneliness had left her soul and were replaced by hope.

"We cannot change the past, no matter how much we want to," Haley's dad said, "But what we can do is to make the best of the future. You have been through so much Haley, more than anyone your age should ever have to go through. You can survive anything life throws at you. Find out what it is you love to do and do it. Look around you. There's a big world out there just waiting to be explored."

"I just wish I was brave and strong like you and mom," Haley said, with tears still in her eyes.

Her father looked down at her and smiled. "You already are."

Haley and her dad went back into the house hand in hand. Haley promised she would never hide her feelings when she felt sad or afraid again. She told him that if she ever had a nightmare, saw the headlights of the truck or felt unsafe again, she would let him know straight away. They were in this together, after all.

Haley knew that it wasn't going to be easy, but she was used to life not being easy, so she was ready for it. She also knew that she wasn't alone. She had a dad who loved her more than anything in the world. From that day on, Haley promised herself that she wouldn't let her past control her life anymore, and that she would do her best to make sure that she would have the best future she possibly could. She had found hope. She could be anyone she wanted to be, and she was finally ready to find out who that was.

Obsessive-Compulsive Disorder (OCD)

Michael's Story

I live with a monster called OCD,
Why can't it just let me be?

Michael was a young boy with dreams. He wanted to be a strong and courageous superhero like Batman or Spiderman. He wanted to write books and live in mansions. He wanted to see the world. He wanted it all. But something was holding him back.

When Michael played football outside he could play for hours on end without ever wanting to stop. He loved playing football and dreamed of playing for Liverpool when he was older. One day, it started to rain. He wanted to go into the house so he wouldn't get wet, but something was holding him back, telling him not to.

For some reason, Michael felt that if he didn't do at least seven keepie-uppies before going inside his house that his house would burn down! Michael could easily do more than seven keepie-uppies but if he did more, he would have to start all over again. "I have to save my house. If it goes on fire it will be all my fault," he said to himself as he kicked the ball in the air. When he finally got seven – exactly seven, no more or no less, and without cheating by stopping when he could have continued, he finally allowed himself to go back inside the house. He felt relieved it was over but confused that it had happened at all.

When Michael went to bed that night and was turning off the light, his mind told him to turn it back on and back off – again and again. If he didn't turn it on and off ten times, a ghost would come into his room while he was asleep and take him away! 'I can feel the ghost watching me from outside the window!' Michael thought to himself, as he flicked the switch on and off. 'I can't let it take me away from my house.' When he finally got into bed, Michael worried about why he kept getting the feeling that something bad was going to happen.

In the morning, Michael went to the bathroom to wash his hands. When he washed and dried them, he got the feeling that they were still dirty. He washed them again, and again, and again. The more he washed them, the more his mind told him they weren't clean.

"Why aren't they clean? How can I make them clean?" he sighed, as he rubbed his hands with soap.

"Your hands are still dirty," Michael's mind hissed. "If you go out now they will still be dirty and everything you touch will get dirty. And it will be all your fault. Do you want that? Do you want everything to get dirty because you didn't clean your hands?"

Michael washed and washed his hands until he felt they were clean. When he finally left the bathroom, he felt confused and embarrassed over what had just happened.

Michael couldn't understand why he was having all of these thoughts. "Am I going mad?" he asked himself. He was afraid that if he told anyone about his thoughts, they would think that he was crazy and he would be taken away from his home and locked away. At lunchtime in school, Michael began to avoid playing with his friends. When Merlyn and Steve asked him to play football, he told them he couldn't because he had a sore foot. But that was a lie. What he was really doing was avoiding stepping on all of the cracks on the pavement. 'If I step on one, there will be an earthquake,' he thought. He had to make sure that he avoided all the cracks to stop the earthquake from happening.

Months passed and the thoughts in Michael's head only got stronger. They told him something bad was going to happen unless he did something about it. If he tried to ignore them, they would only get louder until he obeyed them.

Every morning, Michael would have to walk out of his room in a particular way. If he ever stepped on a stone while he was walking outside, he would have to step on it again. He would often touch or tap objects like doors, walls or tables until things felt 'just right'. Sometimes when he was in the car and the car drove over a pothole, Michael would worry that they had hit a dog! Even though there was no dog and he could see that there was no dog there, Michael would still worry that the car had hit one. At school, he could only write with a black pen. If he used a different colour, his mind would tell him that something bad was going to happen.

Michael kept all these thoughts to himself. He thought he was the only one to have these kind of thoughts. He thought that if he told anyone, they would think that he was crazy and that they would take him away forever. And he couldn't let that happen.

Over time, the thoughts in Michael's head grew worse and worse. Michael couldn't even drink out of the same cups as everyone else in his house. One day, he went to the supermarket and bought five cups – three for coffee and two for tea. Then he told everyone in the house that they were his cups and no one else in the house was allowed to use them. One day, his mother drank from one of his cups because she forgot it was Michael's. When Michael saw this, he panicked! 'If I drink out of this cup now, I'll get sick!' he thought.

That night when no one else was in the kitchen, Michael took the cup that his mother had used out of the dishwasher and threw it on the floor. He collected the tiny pieces and emptied them into the bin. 'If I can't drink from it, no one can,' he thought. He went to bed that night feeling disappointed with himself and confused. He knew deep down that nothing bad would happen if someone drank out of one of his cups. He ate from the same plates and drank from the same glasses as everyone else did, after all. But he couldn't shake off the feeling that if he did drink from the same cups as everyone else, he would get sick for a very long time. "Better safe than sorry," he said to himself.

Michael became so frightened of the thoughts in his head that he stayed at home as often as he could. He would clean the kitchen in his house for hours at night, often cleaning past four o'clock in the morning. He would avoid going outside, because he felt that if he went outside he would get sick. He wore gloves, not because his hands were cold, but because he was so afraid of touching something that would make them dirty and give him dangerous germs. He couldn't walk on the cracks on the road. People on the street must have thought he looked so silly, hopping over the cracks as he walked through the town!

Michael's life had become a living hell.

Michael couldn't take it anymore. He had to tell somebody that he kept thinking that something bad was going to happen if he didn't do anything to stop it, but who? He decided he would go to the doctor. Surely he'd know what was going on? But he couldn't just go to the doctor without a reason. "I know!" he said, "I'll tell my parents that I hurt my foot playing football. Then I'll be able to go and see the doctor!"

The next day, Michael went to the doctor with his parents and asked if he could go in alone.

"Oh, alright," his mam said, "but I'll be right outside here waiting for you."

"Hello Michael, how are you today?" asked the doctor.

"I'm doing okay, but..." and Michael started crying. He told the doctor everything. He couldn't keep this secret to himself anymore. He thought he was going crazy and he didn't want to be taken away from his family and locked away.

"You're not going crazy," the doctor said. "It sounds to me like you have OCD. It means you worry a little more than everyone else."

"OCD?" Michael asked, curious to know more.

"It stands for Obsessive Compulsive Disorder," the doctor replied. "Sometimes people with OCD get a feeling that something bad will happen and you can't get rid of that feeling. This is called an obsession. In your mind the only way to stop this bad thing from happening is to do something called a compulsion, like washing your hands or turning the light switch on and off. Sometimes people with OCD need to have everything perfect and in order. If they feel something is not perfect, they will get anxious and won't feel better until they fix it. Some people are obsessed with numbers or letters. There are many different ways OCD shows itself to the world."

"That's just like me!" Michael exclaimed, relieved to hear that the doctor understood what was going on in his head. "So, I'm not crazy?" he asked, a little less worried now that he knew there were other people with OCD, just like him.

"You're not crazy," smiled the doctor. "You're just going to have to be brave, accept it and not run away from it. Facing up to your struggles is half the battle."

That day, Michael learned a lot about OCD and how it affected people around the world.

"A lot of people think OCD is just washing your hands over and over and being really clean and tidy," explained the doctor, "but it's much more than that. There are many different forms. Some people might see someone with OCD who has a messy room and think to themselves, 'He doesn't have OCD! His room is too messy!' But the people who say this are wrong. That same person may wash his hands a lot, may not be able to step on the cracks on a footpath or may have to check to see if the door is locked, over and over. I know a little girl who can't write down the number three in her copybook because she is so frightened of it. I'll say it again. OCD shows itself in many different ways. And this will be important to remember when you are fighting it."

When Michael got home that day, he said to himself, "OCD! OCD! Three little letters. That doesn't seem so scary! I'm going to be brave. I'm going to fight this and I'm going to beat it! I don't want to be afraid anymore. I'm not going to let OCD control my life. And I want to stop OCD from hurting anyone who has it."

And Michael did fight it. It was really difficult, but he remembered what the doctor told him that day when he found out about OCD, that facing up to your problems is half the battle. And he never ran away from the monster that is OCD, ever again. Do you know how I know that? He wrote this book that you have in your hands right now! And if he can be strong and stand up to OCD and fight it, so can you.

Rules to Follow for Better Overall Mental Health

Exercise daily

Exercise every day. Exercise releases feel-good chemicals called endorphins, which trigger feelings of happiness. It reduces stress and boosts your self-confidence. It helps strengthen your joints and bones. It even improves your creativity – many of my ideas for this book came to me while I was walking my dog! My suggestion would be to find a sport you enjoy doing and do it. Make sure you try to exercise every day, even if it's just walking your dog for thirty minutes to an hour.

Eat Healthy Food

Eating the right food will boost your mood and energy. Eat lots of fruits and vegetables. Eat healthy carbohydrates like bread, pasta and rice. Make sure that you're eating an adequate amount of protein, carbohydrates and fats. Limit the amount of junk food you eat, but there's no need to cut them out completely. You deserve to treat yourself every now and then! Most importantly, don't go on any extreme diets. If you want your body to function well, you need to feed it the right kind of food.

Drink Plenty of Water Every Day

It is extremely important for both your mind and body that you stay hydrated. It is very common to feel stressed or have a headache due to not staying hydrated during the day. Water helps to maintain energy levels. It also helps your skin to look clear and healthy and strengthens your immune system. My advice would be to take a bottle of water with you wherever you go to drink throughout the day.

Exercise Your Mind

Like your body, your mind needs exercise too. Writing, drawing or learning to play an instrument are great ways to improve your creativity. Reading is an excellent way to improve your concentration and reduce stress. Set challenges for your brain to keep it active and stress-free, like doing a puzzle, a crossword or playing chess.

Get a Healthy Amount of Sleep

Sleep is crucial for your overall mental health. Lack of sleep can cause irritability and stress and can lead to depression or anxiety down the road. Sleep is essential for both your mind and body and it is important for growth, repair and energy levels. In order to function at your very best, you need an adequate amount of sleep.

Set Goals

Plan for the future. Write down what you want to accomplish within the day, week, month and year. This will help to give you a sense of purpose in life. When you feel as if you want to give up you can look back on the goals you wrote down and see how far you've come and use that as motivation to keep going.

Be You

Do what you want to do in life, not what others want you to do. It's your life and they're your dreams. Don't let somebody's opinion of what you want to do in life stop you from doing it.

Be Grateful for what You Have

Focus on what you do have and not on what you don't have. Life is a gift. Don't waste it by complaining about all the bad things in your life. Instead, be grateful for all the good things you have.

Eliminate Anything that Brings Stress and Negativity into Your Life

If there is someone or something out there affecting your mood for the worse, cut it or them out – you don't need it in your life. You deserve to live a happy life. If people are trying to bring you down for no reason or if something is changing your life for the worse and not for the better, let go and move on.

Try New Things

Always look to grow as a person. Never settle for being the person you are when you could become so much more. Take up new hobbies, meet new people, visit different places. Always look to challenge yourself – even if that challenge scares you.

Be Here Now

Stop worrying about what the future may hold or being miserable over something you cannot change from the past. Depression lives in the past while anxiety waits for you in the future. Live in the now, where life is what you make it.

Giving is Better than Receiving

It is always better to give than to receive. When you give, it reminds you that you have something to offer the world. It gives you a sense of pride and happiness that is of much greater value to you than whatever you gave away.

My Thoughts on the Mental Health Stigma

We live in a society where the very mention of mental illness makes people look down at the ground and turn their back to you. For some reason, no one wants to admit that mental illness is a very real and major problem in the world today. If you were to break your arm or your leg, you would be told to go to the hospital immediately. Your arm or leg would be put in a cast and you would keep that cast on until your injury had healed. Similarly, if you had a sore throat or a stomach bug you would be told to stay in bed and rest up until you felt better. So it baffles me that mental illness is not treated in the same way. If you were to say that you were feeling down or that you were feeling stressed, you would be told to cheer up and just get on with things. Ignoring the issue will only make things worse in the long run and turning your back on something won't make it go away. In my opinion, we need to speak up about mental illness and put it on the same level of urgency as a physical injury or a physical illness when looking for help.

Advice to People Fighting Mental Illness

Don't Suffer in Silence

My advice to anyone suffering with their mental health is not to suffer in silence. Speak up and tell someone about your issues. You don't always have to act like you're invincible by hiding your pain, and sometimes the bravest thing you can do is to admit that you need help. Nobody likes showing weakness, but the harsh truth is that your life isn't always going to be easy. There will be times when it's difficult and there will even be times when you won't be able to beat your demons on your own. Everyone falls down in life, but not everyone can get back up on their own. If people realize this and see that there is no shame in asking for help to get back to your feet, I believe that people wouldn't have nearly as many issues with their mental health.

Never Give Up

My second piece of advice to anyone struggling with mental health problems is not to give up. Life is going to get hard sometimes. But the challenging times are when you grow and learn the most. I am far stronger right now than I would ever have been without my dark times. If you use the hard times as an opportunity to grow and not give up, you'll become much stronger because of it. If you give up you'll never get better, but if you keep fighting, you will beat whatever demon it is you're fighting and you'll be much stronger because of it.

Remember That You Are Not Your Illness

Don't let your mental illness control you. Your illness is a part of you, but you are so much more than it. Don't let your illness stop you from being who you want to be, doing what you want to do, or going where you want to go. When you don't let your illness control you with fear, there's very little else in life that can frighten you.

Why I Wrote this Book

As someone with my own history of mental health issues, I always kept quiet about my struggles because I afraid that people would think I was weird or crazy. I started experiencing symptoms of OCD and anxiety in general from the young age of five, and depression followed later. I didn't know that mental illness even existed and if I had, I would certainly have sought help for my issues much sooner than I did. I wrote this book to help other people in a way that I was never helped. I hope that everyone reading this book, young and old, can identify with a character in the book and draw strength from their story, whether that's to seek help for their problems or to just find a moment's reassurance. This book is written for people of all ages and I hope you have as much fun reading it as I did writing it.

Poetry on Mental Illness and Questions

❖

Mental Illness Doesn't Care

In this lifetime, we all have a fight,

That we've ignored for too long and have to make right.

If we are to win, we must become one,

It doesn't matter who you are or what you have done.

Our enemy doesn't care where you live, or whether you're black or you're white,

It doesn't care about your gender or your weight or your height.

It doesn't care about your views or religion, and won't ask for your name,

It doesn't care if you're rich or you're poor, or if you've achieved fame.

It doesn't care about your past, or whether you're good or you're bad,

And doesn't even care how you feel, be it happy or sad!

Mental illness doesn't care, it comes for us all,

So don't be ashamed and speak up, this is your call.

Accept Who You Are

Excuse me, my friend, I have a confession,

I hope you don't mind but I've got major depression.

And if I don't talk, or I look very sad,

Just accept my apology and please don't be mad.

And if I alarm you, please forgive me,

For I am often troubled by anxiety.

I don't mean to annoy you, it is not my intention,

My brain has put me on mental detention.

***

Now let's flip the switch, and let me give you advice,

Everyone has days where they don't think they look nice.

And it's not your fault if you're anxious or depressed

Because all that really matters is that you're trying your best.

So stop apologizing if you've not done anything wrong,

You don't have to be perfect if you want to belong.

You are already special, just for being you,

So embrace who you are, it's all you can do.

When I'm Depressed

When I've a sore tummy

I call for my mummy,

She brings me some tea

And takes care of me.

But when I'm depressed

I get up and get dressed.

When I've a sore throat

I give my school a sick note,

I watch movies in bed

And get medicine spoon-fed.

But when I get stressed

I try to hide it my best.

When I feel sad,

They say, 'You don't have it so bad,

And it's a good day,

So come on over and play.'

If only they knew

Then they would feel sad too.

When I'm depressed

I get up and get dressed,

I put on my fake smile

And will keep it on for a while.

But what would you say

If I said that I wasn't okay?

Questions

- Do you think there is anything to be ashamed of if you aren't feeling okay?

- What would you say if someone said sorry to you for being sad?

- Do you agree that you're already special and that you should embrace who you are?

- Do you think mental illness should be treated more seriously like physical illness is?

- When I get stressed I try to hide it my best. Do you think we should tell someone when we are stressed, or should we stay quiet and not say a word?

- But what would you say if I said that I wasn't okay?

- What would you say if your friend said that they weren't okay?

- Do you agree that mental illness can affect everyone equally?

- Do you think we should help each other as a group or focus on ourselves when talking about mental health issues?

- Mental illness doesn't care, it comes for us all. So don't be ashamed and speak up – this is your call. What do these lines mean to you?

Final Thoughts

As I was writing this book, I had the privilege of speaking to people from all over the world, and it helped me to realize just how common mental illness truly is. Mental illness is something that can affect anyone at any time. It doesn't matter who you are, where you're from or what you've done, mental illness doesn't discriminate. Unfortunately, mental illness is something that has remained in the shadows until now, and people have been too afraid to speak up because of the reaction they might receive. Use this book as a guide whenever you're having doubts or feeling alone to remind yourself that you're not. Everyone has a voice, and everyone has a right to use that voice. Mental illness affects us all. Now is the time to come together and use our voices to show the world that mental illness is real. No one need feel ashamed about mental illness ever again.

Acknowledgements

❖

I would like to thank my parents for putting a roof over my head, clothes on my back and food on the table. I couldn't ask for anything more from you both.

Thank you to Mr. John Burns who took the time out of his day to help me arrange a schedule so I would stick to writing and who made sure I kept to it.

Thank you to Dr. Deirdre O'Donnell for reading the book and giving me a psychologist's opinion before giving it to an editor. I would also like to thank her for everything she has done for me and my mental health since our first appointment more than four years ago. I am forever grateful to you.

Thank you to my publisher, Orla Kelly of Orla Kelly Publishing, for helping me publish this book and for offering such a good quality service. Thank you for your personal approach, patience and honesty that ensured this book the is the best version of itself it could possibly be.

Thank you to my editor, Jean O' Sullivan of Red Pen Edits, for making sure that this book was ready for publishing. Thank you for your patience, honesty and being there to answer every question I sent your way, no matter how small. You really went the extra mile for me.

Thank you to Joshua Nueva for designing a front cover that captures everything that this book has to say. It looks better than I ever imagined.

Thank you to everyone who read a story for me and gave me feedback. Without your feedback, it would be a much different book than it is today.

Thank you to everyone who opened up to me and gave me their trust allowing me to learn more about the different types of mental illnesses and how they can manifest, so I could write about them in this book.

Thank you to my dog (yes really), Buddy, for getting up from his bed and coming for late night walks with me so I could plan my stories. Those walks brought me a lot of ideas.

Finally, I would like to thank you, the reader. If you're holding this in your hands right now, thank you so much. I hope there was something in it that was of value to you.

❖ Please Review this Book

Thank you for taking the time to read this book. If you found it helpful, please help me spread the message to others who may be seeking this information. Please visit Amazon, or the platform where you purchased this book to write a review. A review can also be left on Goodreads. This matters because most potential readers first judge a book by what others have to say. An honest review would be most appreciated.

Made in the USA
Monee, IL
05 August 2022

11038480R00111